HINDU WOMEN
and
THE POWER OF IDEOLOGY

HINDU WOMEN

and

THE POWER OF IDEOLOGY

Vanaja Dhruvarajan

BERGIN & GARVEY PUBLISHERS, INC.

MASSACHUSETTS

I gratefully dedicate this book to the people of Musali

First published in 1989 by
Bergin & Garvey Publishers, Inc.
670 Amherst Road   .
Granby, Massachusetts 01033

90   987654321

Printed in the United States of America

Library of Congress Cataloging-in-Publication Data

Dhruvarajan, Vanaja.
    Hindu women and the power of ideology / Vanaja Dhruvarajan.
        p.   cm.
    Bibliography: p.
    Includes index.
    ISBN 0–89789–145–7 (alk. paper) : $39.95
    1. Women, Hindu—India—Social conditions.   2. Sex role—India.
    3. Women in Hinduism   I. Title.
HQ1743.D38 1989
305.4'0882945—dc19   88–28692
                                                       CIP

—CONTENTS—

Preface   *vii*

Chapter I   The Village Setting   *1*

Chapter II   The Author in the Village   *15*

Chapter III   Pativratya: The Ideology   *26*

Chapter IV   Women's Lives within the Family Structure   *35*

Chapter V   The Daily Life of Brahmin and Vokkaliga
                Women   *49*

Chapter VI   Socialization of Women Through the Life Cycle 1:
                Preparation for and Arrangement of Marriage   *58*

Chapter VII   Socialization of Women Through the Life Cycle 2:
                Married Life, Old Age, and Widowhood   *79*

Chapter VIII   Pativratya and Women's Personality   *98*

Chapter IX   Pativratya and the Hindu Woman's Destiny   *108*

Appendix A   Case Histories   *122*

Appendix B   Tables   *150*

Endnotes   *152*

Selected Bibliography   *157*

Index   *165*

PREFACE

The life of Hindu women has intrigued me for a long time. I am fascinated by the richness of Hindu culture that is thousands of years old and the deeply complex Hindu philosophy. At the same time I am disturbed by the ambivalent status accorded to women in Hindu society. Women are held in high regard as mothers but as persons they are utterly devalued. The female principle is worshipped along with the male, but women in flesh and blood are humiliated, depersonalized, and dominated. Instead of outrage at such a state of affairs, there appears to be a silent compliance on the part of Hindu women. Most Hindu men, from upper and lower echelons of the society, seem to have a strong conviction that things are the way they ought to be. I had to know how and why this could be.

My quest to understand the underlying causes of this state of affairs resulted in this book. I have tried to find out how women are made to accept such an ambivalent position and how everyone develops a conviction of the legitimacy of the subordinate position accorded to women. In addition, I have attempted to account for the remarkable stability in the relative position of women and to explain why, in spite of consistent efforts on the part of the enlightened leadership, it has not been possible to alter significantly the position of women in contemporary India.

The study was done in a small village in south India. I not only observed the life-style of villagers in all its facets but also asked the villagers themselves to interpret their lives for me. In this process I tried to assess the underlying motivations by identifying the factors that provided them with inspiration, and through observation analyzed the structures that circumscribed their lives.

There are nine chapters in this book. Chapters 1 and 2 deal with the village setting and the data collection procedure. Chapter 3 delineates the androcentric ideology of Pativratya that provides the ideological climate for the lives of men and women. In chapters 4 to 8, the structural context of women's lives and their socialization experiences are discussed. It is shown how the androcentric ideology is built into the social structure, thereby determining the course of women's lives. Women, in this context, not only accept their subordinate position but become active participants in perpetuating the status quo. Finally, in the last chapter, I have attempted to account briefly for the Hindu women's destiny historically and in contemporary society.

There are many people who have helped me to make the dream of publishing this book come true. Here I mention only those who have helped me directly. I am grateful to many others who have kindly provided assistance to me indirectly.

My sincere gratitude to Professor Greta H. Nemiroff for making many comments and suggestions that were very useful. My thanks to Professors Fred L. Strodtbeck, Mary-Jo Neitz, P. S. Dhruvarajan, Dan Chekki, and G. N. Ramu for commenting on an earlier draft of the manuscript. I would also like to thank Dr. Raghu D. Rajan for proofreading the manuscript and Ms. Judi Hanson for typing it with great efficiency and care.

Finally, I would like to express my deep appreciation to my husband Raj and my sons, Raghu and Prabhu, for all the love and encouragement they have given me over the years.

Chapter I

THE VILLAGE SETTING

The village of Musali is located approximately in the south-central part of the Indian subcontinent. The significant features of life in Musali are the all-pervasive influence of Hinduism and the agricultural way of life. The effects of the process of modernization are felt differently by different segments of the population. Descriptions below give an idea about the nature and tenor of life in this village.

Musali[1] belongs to the *hobli* (an administrative division) of Shanti-grama in the Hassan district of Karnataka State in India. There were 699 people—men, women, and children—residing in the village in 1977. The bus stand that connects Musali with nearby cities and towns is about one mile away and the railway station one and a half miles away. It only takes about twenty minutes to reach Hassan, the district headquarters, by bus or train. As the buses run more frequently than the trains and the bus stand is closer, most villagers use the bus to get to Hassan or Holenarasipur (another nearby town) despite a slightly higher cost per trip.[2] There is one upper primary school with "standards" (grades) one to seven in the village. Children of Musali who go to high school—about six or seven at the time of this study—walk to Hosoor, about one and a half miles from Musali, where the school is located. A hospital with one doctor on duty and two assistants is also located in Hosoor. Many villagers from Musali take advantage of the services available in this hospital for simple ailments. Since Hosoor has no facilities for hospitalization, treatment of complicated diseases, or surgery, villagers must go to the large hospital in Hassan. The nearest post office is also at Hosoor, but the postmaster as well as a letter carrier live in Musali. Stamps, money order forms, and air letters are available from the postmaster, and letters can be mailed using the mail box, located in the center of the village, which is cleared once a day at 10:30 A.M. Money orders can also be sent through the postmaster. People in the village get their mail delivered in the afternoon between 1:30 and 3:30.

CASTE COMPOSITION OF MUSALI

The belief in the hierarchy of castes prevalent all across Hindu India is shared by the villagers. The notions of purity and pollution determine the hierarchy. The Brahmins rank the highest on this scale and are considered to be ritually most pure, followed by Kshatriyas, Vaisyas, and Śudras in descending order of purity. The scheduled castes or untouchables are the outcasts of society. The first three castes—Brahmins, Kshatriyas, and Vaisyas—are considered *dwijas*, twice born, because they have the right to undergo religious initiation. This right is denied to women of all castes and Śudras. In terms of ritual purity, women in each caste are believed to be less pure than the men of their caste. Maintaining caste hierarchy has always been a primary concern, hence the rules pertaining to marriage are strictly adhered to. Marriages in general take place within one's caste. Exceptions can be made in cases where a woman of lower caste marries a man of upper caste. This practice is referred to as *anuloma* marriage. But *pratiloma* marriage, in which a woman of upper caste marries a man of lower caste, is prohibited. Violation of this rule can result in excommunication. The concern here seems to be that an ambivalence in the caste/sex hierarchy will result in the context of *pratiloma* marriages. Some villagers are of the opinion that the untouchables are the products of such marriages.

Higher rank in the caste hierarchy does not automatically mean higher status in terms of economic and political power. In this village only Brahmin and Śudra castes are represented. There are instances where some Vokkaligas, members of a Śudra subcaste, command more political and economic power than some Brahmins. In interpersonal relationships, even though formal respect is accorded to Brahmins by these powerful men, more often than not it lacks in sincerity.

The Brahmin caste consists of more educated people which is true for both men and women (see Appendix B, Table 1 and Table 4). The Vokkaliga (also known as Okkaliga) has the numerical majority, with the Brahmins being second highest, and the scheduled castes (the outcasts, or untouchables) third.[3] Each caste has a number of subcastes *(jātis)* which are socially meaningful. A *jāti* operates as a social group to which a given individual belongs by birth. Social relationships are closer between members of a given *jāti*. As a rule, marital partners are members of the same *jāti*. In the past a given *jāti* indicated a particular occupation which was passed on from one generation to the next. Today, this is only broadly true, because with the availability of new occupations, traditional patterns are not adhered to by everyone.

Jāti extends beyond the confines of any single village. There is a general belief that, similar to castes, the *jātis* are also arranged hierarchically. There are differences of opinion, however, with regard to the precise status of a given *jāti* within the hierarchy. Although the introduction of a money economy, the emergence of caste-free occupations, the free sale of land, and the rise of political parties have all eroded the hierarchical structure, the opportunity structure remains relatively closed to *jātis* in the lower rungs of the social ladder. The upper and middle levels now have almost equal access to economic opportunity. In general, the belief in the legitimacy of the caste system is questioned by only a few, and the social distance between different *jātis* is scrupulously maintained.

As is evident from the above discussion, *jāti* in India is not the exact analogue of class in the Western society. Unlike the class system, membership in a *jāti* is achieved only by birth. But there are similarities. Both members of a given social class and the members of a *jāti* feel a sense of closer affinity. Social intercourse, whether dining together or intermarriage, is more common between the members of the same class and among members of the same *jāti*. Just as for various classes, the opportunity structure for the various *jātis* is also significantly different. One can state that members of a given *jāti*, just as members of a given class, share a common sociocultural milieu.

ECONOMIC STRUCTURE

There is electricity in the village, and all the main streets as well as about two-thirds of the houses in the village have electric lights. Those homes without have remained so because the householders cannot pay for the installation of a meter and wiring—about $50.00. The village also has running tap water. About one-half of the householders have installed faucets inside their houses, and the other half gets its drinking water from the taps located at street intersections.

The village has a dairy, run by a cooperative society, where fresh milk is available every morning and evening. The society buys milk from people in the village and sells as much as possible between 10:00 in the morning and 9:00 at night, at which time the unsold milk is taken to nearby Hosoor, where it is sold.

The village has both a flour mill and a rice mill run by electricity. These mills serve Musali as well as a few other neighboring villages. The charges for milling are considered reasonable by most villagers.[4]

There is a cooperative society operating in Hosoor which provides long-term and short-term loans to villagers for purchasing fertilizer, seeds, or farming equipment for small ventures such as sheep farms, egg farms, or the purchase of milk cows and buffaloes. The loan must be repaid promptly. I found that many villagers from Musali had availed themselves of the opportunity provided by the society but had been tardy in paying back the loans. The high default rate had damaged their credit ratings. Among the reasons for default were crop failures, too many children with consequent heavy household expenditures, or sickness and death in the family. The long-term loan given to the milk cooperative for starting the dairy—a successful venture—is being repaid promptly.

The nature of farming in the village is mixed. The soil is considered fertile, providing wetlands (*gadde*), dry lands (*hola*), and garden lands (*thota*). Rice and sugarcane are grown on wetlands; millet, maize, pulses, spices, and potato on dry lands; and arecanut, coconut, betel leaf, bananas, tamarind, and mango on garden lands. Potato, sugarcane, arecanut, coconut, betel leaf, bananas, and a small portion of pulses and

THIS TANK, LOCATED AT THE EDGE OF THE VILLAGE, SUPPLIES THE DRINKING WATER FOR MUSALI.

spices are the cash crops; the rest of the crops are grown for home consumption. In addition, vegetables are grown in kitchen gardens. The major types of vegetables are various types of squash, eggplant (foreign and domestic varieties), okra, tomato, chili, cucumber, bean, spinach, and coriander. The major types of fruits grown are bananas, melons, jack fruits, papayas, and several varieties of mangoes.

The major source of water for the village is the monsoon rains, there being no canals or rivers to provide a year-round supply. Whenever the monsoons are good, the two village reservoirs get filled up. During those years the more profitable wet crops and garden crops are successful, and the level of economic well-being in the village is correspondingly higher. But if the tanks do not get filled up, as is likely to occur about once every two years, people come close to starvation. The wet crops are completely destroyed, and garden crops shrink to a minimum. If the tanks do not fill up for two years in a row, the arecanut trees, coconut trees, and banana plants also begin to die. The dry crops usually continue to do well as they require less water.

Outdated implements are used to till the soil and harvest the crops; however, some villagers have started to use fertilizers and pesticides consistently. Some pests are well controlled, whereas others, such as monkeys (which damage fruit and coconut crops) and rats (which eat away the grains), are not.

The size of land holdings and the amount of revenue paid to the government indicates that Brahmins are on the average better off than other castes, with Vokkaligas ranking second. It is difficult to calculate the per capita income of the villagers as the income of many people does not easily translate into cash. In addition, since crops are unpredictable, one can obtain only a rough estimate even when the average of several years is taken. Despite this, the population profile, the size of land holdings, and the amount of revenue paid, together with the average family size give us a fairly good idea about the level of economic well-being of the people of Musali (see Appendix B, Table 3).

OCCUPATION

The major occupation in Musali is agriculture. Cattle rearing is also prevalent to the extent of providing for a modest consumption of milk and draught animals to pull the plow. There are some people in the village who supplement their farm income in jobs such as teaching, shopkeeping, tailoring, or village administration. One group of people called Agasas (a Śudra subcaste), who traditionally earned a living by washing clothes in other peoples' houses, are virtually without jobs now. Villagers do their own washing since most are unable to pay the Agasas their yearly ration in farm produce. There are three such families in the village, all of whom depend on farm labor or other kinds of work to make a living.

Those people who are landless—about fifteen families—and those who do not own enough land to support their families work part-time in other peoples' farms or take up jobs that are available on a temporary basis like road construction or repair work on the village reservoir. A silk farm is being planned two miles from the village, and people were hurrying to add their names to the list of available laborers. There were some Muslims (those who adhere to the Islamic faith) who earned a living exclusively through making *beedi* (leaf cigarettes that are popular in rural areas). As this has become less profitable many have left the village to settle in the nearby city of Hassan.

Some families leave the village as their sons obtain better jobs in cities or pursue further education. The daughters of many families leave the village after getting married. The male population is slightly higher than the female population, similar to the national sex composition. The average family size is approximately six for all castes, Muslims and Vokkaligas having larger families than Brahmins and other castes (see Appendix B, Table 2).

A YOUNG VOKKALIGA WOMAN TENDS TO A MILKING BUFFALO.

RELIGION

Apart from fifteen Muslims almost all others in the village belong to the Hindu faith. Muslims are followers of Islam religion. According to villagers these people were originally Śudras but got converted several hundred years ago. These people stay away from all the ceremonies and rituals related to Hinduism. They, as a group, occupy a lower position in the social hierarchy. It is at least partly because their numbers are small and they are not economically well off. The Lingayats consider themselves non-Hindus as this movement started as a rebellion against Hinduism. But they still have not rejected any of the beliefs of Hinduism and probably rank closer to Brahmins in their orientation towards life.

There are several temples in the village, of which two (Keshava and Shiva) are recognized by the Tourist Department of the central government. In theory, all Hindu temples are accessible to all castes. In practice, however, different castes patronize different temples: Brahmins—Keshava; Lingayat—Shiva; Vokkaliga—Hanuman; scheduled castes—Mariyamma. The Muslims used to have a Musjid (same as Mosque) of their own, but as several families have moved to nearby towns, the Musjid is no longer operating. For religious service, they now must go to Hassan. Two scheduled-caste watchmen have been hired to protect the temples from vandalism and keep the surroundings neat and clean. There is also one temple curator, a Brahmin, who is responsible for keeping the inside of the Keshava and Shiva temples clean and neat and performs daily worship. All of these people are paid by the central government. Another temple, which is for the god Hanuman, is taken care of by a Brahmin curator who gets his remuneration from a small plot of land reserved for the temple. The temple of Gramadevatha (the village goddess) is taken care of by a non-Brahmin curator who gets his remuneration from periodic payments made by the villagers. A stone image of the goddess Mariyamma, patronized by those of scheduled castes, stands by itself in the outskirts of the village without any wall around it.

All castes worship Gramadevatha. Brahmins are allowed to go into the inside sanctum of any temple, but all other castes usually stand outside and pray. Even though it is now a legal right of scheduled castes to enter and worship in any temple, most of them do not exercise this right. Since the appointment of the two scheduled-caste watchmen in the Shiva and Keshava temples, Brahmin attendance in these temples has dwindled. As none of the upper-caste people defy the government, these watchmen are allowed to continue in their jobs, but whenever the Brahmins come to visit the temple the watchmen stay at a respectful distance.

LANGUAGE

The major language spoken by the people of Musali is Kannada, which is the language everyone understands. In addition to this a dialect related to Tamil is spoken exclusively by a group of Brahmin families. The Muslims speak Urdu. Very few people—only about fifteen Brahmins—understand English to the extent of writing simple sentences. Of the 625 adults in Musali, 171 are illiterate.

EATING HABITS

The Brahmins and Lingayats in the village are vegetarians and teetotalers. Other villagers eat meat, although Muslims do not eat pork, and Hindus, for whom the killing of cattle is a taboo, do not eat beef. Those of scheduled castes are allowed to eat the meat of dead cattle. The alcohol consumption in the village is limited to the local brew called "toddy," distilled from a palm tree. The men from scheduled castes are known to drink more than any others. Women in general do not consume alcohol.

STATUS RELATIONSHIPS

Three important criteria that determine social status are caste, age, and sex. Caste hierarchy is clearly established. The criterion of age as an indicator of status is operative mainly within each caste group since caste, being a more powerful criterion, takes precedence over age. With regard to sex, the same holds true. Between age and sex, sex seems to be a more important factor, taking precedence over age.

Time has eroded the importance of deference customs in establishing status relationships between certain categories like age and caste.[5] Since Independence (1947) the structural changes that have taken place in Indian society have led to a redefinition of relationships. Age and caste have declined as effective criteria of status definition. Introduction of new criteria such as education has disrupted the old definitions. And, the change in the political structure based on an egalitarian value orientation has further diminished the importance of caste and age. A system in which class is based on achievement of political and economic power has broken through the caste boundaries and made the relationships between various caste groups ambiguous.

The deference customs in the arenas of speaking, walking, and sitting behavior do not hold any longer between different castes, except where the scheduled castes are concerned. In sitting and walking behaviors, distance is maintained even though absolute hierarchy is not always adhered to. The distance is maintained to avoid ritual pollution between Brahmins and scheduled castes. With regard to eating behavior, however, the hierarchical principle is still strictly observed.[6] That is, a lower-caste person may eat what the upper-caste person has served, but the reverse does not occur, because of fear of ritual pollution. Brahmins and Lingayats avoid participating fully in community functions like Gramadevatha's (village deity) worship for the same reason.

Within a given sex category, age plays an important role in determining the relationship. Older women, especially when they become mothers-in-law, command respect from younger women. For men such is not always the case, as younger men often defy the older men. This is mainly due to the fact that younger men are becoming better educated and more competent in exerting influence in the political arena.

Women do not generally engage in intercaste relationships. If they do at all, it is only with women of other castes, as strict gender segregation across castes is observed. At times, when intergender encounters happen by chance, avoidance techniques are used. For example, a woman may move to another room to avoid facing a man from another caste. The restrictions are more severe in cases where an upper-caste woman encounters a lower-caste man than in the reverse case.

Deference customs still play a prominent role in relationships between the sexes. These customs have been incorporated into the daily life of each person and are observed as a matter of course. It has become a sign of good breeding, particularly for women. Eligibility of brides is discussed on the basis of the finesse and elegance that the girl displays in the practice of these customs.

SANSKRITIZATION

There seems to be a tendency among the educated and more affluent Vokkaligas to take on the behavioral patterns of Brahmins. This tendency has been called the process of Sanskritization (Srinivas 1968). This is especially evident in the areas of marriage and treatment of women. The system of bride price was in practice in the past among the Vokkaligas. The practice nowadays is dowry, though the amount of money paid to the groom by the bride's side is not as large as among the Brahmins. The amount of dowry expected and given varies in direct proportion to the groom's educational qualification and level of economic status, just as among Brahmins. In both castes the marriage expenses are paid by the bride's father.

In the past, Vokkaliga women had relatively more freedom of movement and speech. This is still true in those families where members have not become "sophisticated," that is, are not behaving like Brahmins. Those among Vokkaligas who consider themselves sophisticated restrict their wives' freedom of movement and speech. Wives require permission to visit neighbors and friends. They can speak only when spoken to and are expected to be docile and retiring. The people in these families feel very proud and look down upon other Vokkaliga families who have retained old traditions in which a woman stood up for her rights at least occasionally. The families that have changed are economically better off and are those in which at least one member has completed high school.

RESIDENTIAL PATTERN

Each caste has its own residential area. The scheduled castes live in the outskirts of the village and are not allowed to move about in the residential area of other communities, except in instances where there is no other route open to them to reach their place of business or another village. For example, the main road in the village runs through the Brahmin residential area, and one must take that road to go to the village school and to the neighboring villages. Sometimes, if a member of the scheduled castes is working as a hired hand in the family of a Vokkaliga, he is allowed to come and go there. The Brahmins as a rule do not employ scheduled castes as hired hands to work near their homes, but allow them to work only in the fields. That they are not welcome is made clear to scheduled caste people repeatedly through nasty looks, verbal abuse, and threat of physical punishment. The Muslims live in one part of the village separated from other religious groups. The Vokkaligas and the Lingayats live in different residential areas, close to each other, with some overlap. There are two Lingayat families living in the Vokkaliga area and two Vokkaliga families near Lingayat households. The Brahmins live in a completely separate area.

People generally mix only with those of their own caste or religion. The children of each caste play among themselves. The only exceptions are found in cases of Vokkaliga and Lingayat children who occasionally mix with each other; this is generally disapproved of by Lingayat parents who consider themselves superior to Vokkaligas. Visiting patterns also are most frequent between members of the same *jāti*. A person of lower caste may sometimes visit the house of an upper-caste person for business or to work in that house. But social visits are strictly between members of the same *jāti*. This rule is more strictly adhered to by women than by men. In an emergency, an upper-caste man may visit the lower-caste home but not the homes of scheduled castes, who are completely excluded and for whom no exceptions are made. Eating is even more rigorously restricted to members of the same *jāti*. In exceptional circumstances, members of a lower caste may eat the food prepared by upper-caste families.

COMMUNITY ACTIVITIES IN THE VILLAGE

The village as a whole participates in the worship of the village deity, Gramadevatha. Each caste participates in its own way according to its position in the social hierarchy. The annual worship of the village goddess is believed necessary to ensure the welfare of the village. Gramadevatha is the guardian deity of the village and must be appeased every year. This is precisely the reason that the whole village is expected to participate. The actual celebration consists of worship, animal sacrifices, a procession, and a feast. This is all taken care of by the Vokkaliga community using funds and material provided by the village, with the labor supplied by the scheduled castes. The meal is served to the Vokkaliga community, and leftovers are given to the scheduled castes. The other communities do not partake in this meal for various reasons. The Muslims do not eat the meal as it is against their religion to celebrate a Hindu festival. The Brahmins and Lingayats do not, as they are vegetarians and also fear ritual pollution.

In terms of monetary contribution, the principle followed is ability to pay. The responsibility of running the function successfully falls on the shoulders of Vokkaligas, the numerically and politically dominant group. Brahmins only participate in the honoring of the diety when the procession goes to each house by making contributions in cash or kind. The animal sacrifice that is made every year is taken care of by the Vokkaligas. Other communities—the Lingayats, scheduled castes, and Muslims—also participate but their role is rather limited. The Muslims, being of a different faith, give only a token contribution in cash. The scheduled castes help in cleaning and doing various required menial chores. The deity is not taken into the scheduled castes' residential area due to fear of pollution or to the Muslim residential area since they are not Hindus. The Lingayats make contributions in cash and kind but do not play an active role in the worship itself.

In addition to worship of the village deity, each caste has its own festivals, all of which have a religious connotation. The ones common to all castes are Ramanavami, Deepavali, Sankranti, Shasti, and Pitri Paksha. These festivals usually coincide with the harvest or sowing seasons. Generally the focus in these festivals is on keeping away evil spirits, protecting the health of the cattle, ensuring regular and sufficient rainfall, honoring and remembering ancestors, or protecting the health of the people.

The Brahmins tend to be more religiously oriented, and their various festivals signify auspicious occasions for the worship of various deities.

Sometimes the aim is to protect the soul and at other times to appease the diety to ensure health and happiness in this world. There are more celebrations focusing on the former rather than the latter, though both objectives are evident in every case. For the Vokkaligas, worldly happiness is usually the desired end.

In addition to festivals there are various life-cycle ceremonies performed by each community, the Brahmins having more of them than the others. Participation in these functions is restricted to members of one's own *jāti*.

VILLAGE GOVERNMENT

A Panchayat council (or village government body), for each group of villages of about 5,000 people, is responsible for civil administration. Eleven members represent Musali and its surrounding villages. It is mandatory that at least one woman be elected. Even though both men and women disapprove of this regulation, a token woman is elected, and she usually plays a very insignificant role in the decision-making process. I

THE LONE WOMAN MEMBER OF MUSALI'S PANCHAYAT (COUNCIL) SITS AT THE FAR LEFT.

spoke with the female representative who was on the council at the time of my study and found her to be a docile woman who firmly believed that men should make all decisions and that the political arena is not for women. She is there because she was asked to do a favor by the chairman of the Panchayat council. I found that another woman who was contesting in the elections was assertive and very desirous of playing an active role in the council. Despite this both men and women voted the docile woman into office precisely because, they said, the former was not feminine enough to represent women.

Administration of justice, criminal or civil, is not under the council's jurisdiction. The important functions of the council are taking care of rural sanitation, supply of clean water and electricity, the collecting of land revenue as well as water and light charges, overseeing the implementation of development projects like road building or repairing the village reservoir to stop or minimize water seepage, keeping an eye on the functioning of school and conduct of teachers, assessment of the developmental needs of the village and reporting them to the district authorities, licensing the various industries operating in the village and insuring their smooth functioning, listening to complaints from villagers on any aspect of village life under the council's jurisdiction and attempting to remedy the cause (for example, people can complain to the council if the school is not functioning properly or if an unscrupulous industrialist is taking advantage of villagers), devising various programs to collect money to improve the quality of life in the village, making certain that milk sold in the dairy is fresh and unadulterated, taking care of distribution of excess municipal land to the landless, and the reporting of all disputes—civil or criminal—to the police and courts so that proper justice is meted out. Programs like adult education or *Mahila Samaj* (women's society) can be initiated by the Panchayat if it has sufficient funds. If funds are not available, it can solicit aid from the district headquarters by making a proper representation of the need for such programs. In Musali the council members lacked such initiative. Except for the nursery school which was running intermittently, nothing much was being done. Except for the treasurer, the secretary, and their assistant no other council member, including the chairman, is paid a salary. The positions carry with them tremendous prestige, however, and therefore there is intense politicking during the period of election to the council.

The dominant castes, the Vokkaligas and the Brahmins, have most representation on the council. The competition for election into office is intense, and the voters look at not only the caste background but also at the competence and programs put forth by the candidates. In this council most of the members belonged to the Vokkaliga caste.

In addition to the Panchayat council recognized by the state and central governments, the traditional "village Panchayat," an informal organization, still exists. It plays a role in mediating disputes between individuals and groups which otherwise would have to be referred to courts. As this organization does not have the official sanction or the support of all villagers, its role is becoming less and less important in village life.

Chapter II

THE AUTHOR IN THE VILLAGE

All the necessary data were collected during my five-month stay in the village in 1977 using methods of observation, participant observation, interviewing, questionnaire, and sentence completion. My book focuses on the Brahmins and the Vokkaligas, a Śudra subcaste, since they are the dominant castes of the village in terms of numbers and of political power. They also represent the top and bottom of the caste hierarchy. I obtained information from at least 200 people in the village and observed at least 300 people, all of whom were either Brahmin or Vokkaliga, in their daily life. I interviewed in a systematic manner about ten men and thirty women among the Brahmins, as well as about fifteen men and forty-five women among the Vokkaligas. Background information was collected from forty-six women, twenty-three Brahmin and twenty-three Vokkaligas (see Appendix A).

The Brahmins in this sample belong either to the Karnataka or Sanketi *jāti*. The main difference between these is that the latter speak a kind of Tamil dialect at home whereas the former speak Kannada only. In this book these two subcastes are combined into one group and referred to as "Brahmins." The frequency of social interaction such as interdining and mutual visits is much greater between them, compared with people belonging to other *jātis*. Marriage, however, generally takes place only within each *jāti*.

The Vokkaligas are a Śudra subcaste. In this village they belong either to the Mullokkalu or the Dasokkalu subcaste. There are some minor differences between these groups in terms of life-style. Mullokkalu people, although they consume meat, are not allowed to cook it in the kitchen area but must do it outside. They are also forbidden from consuming any liquor except brandy. Dasokkalu people do not have any such restrictions. Both are referred to as "Vokkaligas" in this book since, again except for marriage, all other types of social interaction are more frequent between these two subcastes, compared with that of others in the village.

Macro level data were collected mainly from the men. I could interview them with ease and ask various questions, to which answers were given readily. Data on land holdings, amount of revenue paid by each family, and similar economic data were obtained from the village treasurer. Data on village government, crops, and intercaste relationships were obtained through interviews with several men from both castes. The village census was used to obtain data on educational level, age, sex, caste composition, the use of hospitals, and migration patterns. Family planning data were obtained from the doctor at Hosoor, the nearby village. Data on schooling were obtained from school authorities, milk dairy data from the manager of the dairy, and flour mill data from the proprietor.

In the beginning, women felt a little uncomfortable about my presence in their midst. I tried my best to look and dress like them and even participated in their activities during ceremonial occasions, if I was asked to. After a while they accepted me and invited me to their homes whenever there was some special occasion such as the christening of a baby, a girl's first menstruation, marriage, or a thread ceremony for religious initiation. Whenever I asked for permission to stay and watch their daily activities, they readily allowed me to do so. This was true of both Brahmin and Vokkaliga women. I was included in their gossip sessions, song sessions, arecanut and tamarind curing, life-cycle ceremonies, and religious festivals. They often felt intrigued that I considered their activities interesting. They answered my questions willingly and talked into my tape recorder. Many of them opened their hearts to me about their personal troubles even when they knew I could not be of much help. Somehow, in spite of my status, they felt a kind of affinity towards me, probably feeling that as a woman I must be going through the same experiences. Especially in the areas of husband-wife relationships, the general predicament of being a woman, and concern about children, most of them felt that I could empathize. They often corrected my "awkward" behavior whenever it became too obvious. For example, asking questions like "Do wives beat their husbands?" or "Why can't women sit among men after the meals instead of running around cleaning up the place?" or "Why don't they serve the sweets to women first?" were considered inappropriate.

AUTHOR'S RELATIONSHIP TO THE SUBJECT MATTER

I was born and brought up in this village until the age of thirteen. Even though I have been away from the village since then, I have kept contact through periodic visits. While doing field research in one's own culture, one is often classified as either an Insider or an Outsider by various segments of the population at different times.[1] I was considered an Insider since I shared the cultural script with the villagers. But they were ambivalent about my position when confronted with my personal attributes. Thus I became an Outsider when they realized that I have different convictions and loyalties. Those aspects that played an important role in determining my position as an Insider or an Outsider will be discussed in detail. Such a discussion is useful, as one must devise various strategies to collect different types of data, taking into account the sensitivity of the issues involved and also whether one is considered as an Insider or an Outsider.

Having lived in the same village for the first thirteen years of my life provided me with many advantages while I was doing field research. I knew the language, shared many cultural symbols, and could communicate with the villagers with relative ease. Although I had to ask my respondents to objectify their life situation and interpret it for me, my familiarity with their cultural script and social structure helped me to understand them easily, and they did not have to try very hard to make me understand their perceptions and evaluations. In other words, I did not have the kinds of problems researchers unfamiliar with the language and culture would have had.[2]

Srinivas's suggestion that one should start doing field research in a community other than one's own is well taken (1968:255). However, I think this is necessary in particular for those who are immersed in the culture they want to study and need a certain amount of distance to observe meaningfully and report the factual details. Living away from India for almost seventeen years, along with a conscious and deliberate effort toward objectivity, helped me to develop such a distance. My familiarity with the culture made it possible for me to give greater depth to my field research.

Gaining entry into the village was not difficult; in fact, it was the easiest part. I was welcomed with enthusiasm at a specially arranged function, with the traditional garlanding, speech making, and distribution of sweets. The villagers were proud of me and my achievements. The simplicity of my dress and mannerisms, as well as my unassuming attitude, were praised. They felt flattered that I chose this particular village for my study.

The fact that I knew many prominent members of the community was immensely helpful in making the entry into the village. My explanation that the intended research will be studied by people in North America stirred their curiosity. They were intrigued to find out that people in such a far-off place wanted to know about them. I was assured of full cooperation and was told to make myself at home and ask for help from anyone I wanted.

My genuine interest in the welfare of the villagers showed through in many ways, thereby convincing them that I was a friend. I was overjoyed when I saw that the village reservoir was filled with monsoon rain, because this meant a continuous supply of food for most villagers for the whole year. My distress was evident when I heard stories about how many crops had been destroyed during the past drought season. I was irritated to learn that pests were eating away precious grain and monkeys the coconuts, that thieves were pilfering the coconut and banana crops of many people. I was concerned about the marriage of young girls in the village, the education of the children ... well, the list is endless. I felt a strong sense of affinity to them and wished very sincerely that their lives would become better.

I also had some other advantages. First of all, a married woman has a better status, and this is elevated even further if she has sons. Fortunately for me, I have a husband and two sons, and this made me absolutely respectable. Those people who wondered about what I was doing in the village without caring for my family as a proper woman should were relieved to hear that I had gone there with my husband's permission and that my children were old enough to be left under the care of my mother-in-law. Many of them were surprised that I wanted to go through all the hardship of living in a village, when I had everything that a woman needs or desires.

PERSONAL ATTRIBUTES AND FIELD RESEARCH

Being a member of the Brahmin caste and being a woman affected in some ways the kind of data I could collect. There were certain types of data that were completely out of my reach, and for others I had to work very carefully. The data on the sexual behavior and attitudes of men could not be collected directly. I found out that it is inconceivable for a woman to talk about such things with a man. It would have hurt my standing in the village completely if I had tried to collect such data, and this would have effectively put a stop to my research in that village.

I could not observe the interaction between men directly, as I was not allowed to attend most of their gatherings. Apart from observing a few gossip sessions from a distance I could not join them in any other gatherings. Since the sexes were always segregated, my presence among men used to be very conspicuous, and this inhibited normal behavior among them. Very often my presence was either disapproved or prevented. I tried to break a few rules in the beginning but noticed that there was strong resistance. So I hired a young man as my informer, an alternate strategy which worked quite well.

There were some personal problems I had to cope with. The main ones were being away from my family, getting used to a different diet as well as eating schedule, becoming used to living in dark surroundings particularly after sundown, tolerating unclean surroundings with insects like ants and cockroaches commonly present. The first month was the hardest. I made three trips out of the village during the weekends just to make sure that my family was being taken care of properly, as well as to escape from the village. Gradually I became used to the surroundings. As the people were very friendly and helpful, adjustment came easily. Nevertheless it made many villagers feel that I did not really fit in their midst.

My decision to stay in my uncle's house had some drawbacks. First of all, it did not have electric lighting. Second, my uncle's family did not have amicable relationships with some families, and initially this restricted my movements. But gradually I worked my own way through and overcame the restrictions. In spite of these problems I think that the decision was the right one under the circumstances. The idea of renting a house and living there by myself was discarded quickly; this would have been an extremely improper act for a married woman. Any such act on my part would have permanently closed my entry into the community. I thought of inviting someone to live with me, but finding one acceptable to tradition was not easy. The only such person in the circumstances would have been my mother; this was not possible, however, since she had the heavy responsibility of running a large family in the city of Bangalore which is some distance away from the village.

There was some disapproval expressed by Brahmins towards my going into the Vokkaliga residential area to collect data, as it was considered improper for a Brahmin woman to enter their residential area. I certainly did not want to antagonize anyone and had to find a way to solve this problem. I thought it best to collect the data in the Brahmin community first. I then started talking about the need to collect the data from the Vokkaligas as well. Gradually, as the duration of my stay in the village increased, I was able to give convincing reasons to justify the necessity of speaking to Vokkaligas and got approval from my uncle, subject to the condition that I was accompanied by another person whenever I went into the Vokkaliga residential area. I took my female cousin along and began making rounds. After I did this several times, I went alone just to observe the reaction. Nobody seemed to mind it, so I continued. Of course, whenever I had to go there during the evening,

I had to be accompanied by a male assistant; women are not allowed to go out of the house after dark unless accompanied by an adult male.

The Vokkaligas thought of me primarily as a Brahmin woman and only secondarily as a research scientist. Many felt flattered that I, a Brahmin, went to their homes to learn about their way of life. Some others were a little suspicious of me, not knowing what I was up to. Still others felt very shy and diffident about themselves, or they were not sure that they could answer the questions of a more educated woman. I talked to several important men in the community and explained how the help of their women was essential for the completion of my study. Once the first few women complied, others followed readily. While I met with them, they took great care to protect me from becoming ritually polluted.[3] Whenever they were in the same room with me, they made sure that their children did not touch me. They gave me a separate mat, stool, or chair to sit on. They never offered any cooked food, as a Brahmin is not supposed to eat anything cooked by a non-Brahmin. I was offered only milk and fruits, which are considered to be nonpolluting food. I did not want to disrupt this order of things and confuse the issues even though I personally do not believe in them. It also would have gotten me into trouble with the Brahmins if I had broken any rules, and the Vokkaligas would have looked down upon me for not sticking to the Dharma[4] of my caste. They always addressed me with respect, and I accordingly addressed them with the same respect. This was unexpected but was accepted with gratitude. Addressing a person of lower caste with respect is again an improper act. The impropriety involved however is not of a high order, and my indiscretion went unnoticed.

I followed various strategies to collect different types of data, moving cautiously in the beginning and collecting the least controversial macro level data first. During that time I made friends with people of both castes. When I felt that I was accepted and my credibility was established I started taping my interviews. I taped the Brahmins first and then the Vokkaligas, as I needed a little more time to make an entry into the Vokkaliga community. They also needed a little more reassurance from their men that what I was doing was not meant to make fun of them or use them for bad ends. I observed the women's daily routine afterwards, by staying around and watching them at work. They were self-conscious in my presence at first but gradually learned to ignore me. I observed most of the major festivals, attended some life-cycle ceremonies, and collected data on attitudes towards sexual behavior in the end. I also took photographs during the tail end of my stay, as many were too shy to pose for the camera in the beginning.

Familiarity with the village and personal acquaintances among prominent members of the community had certain disadvantages as well. In the first few weeks several prominent villagers took it upon themselves to explain to me the difficult situation the village was in. It appeared that they expected me to be of some help to them. They were worried about the unpredictable monsoons, the problems of pests and theft. More importantly, several upper-caste men were very disturbed by the deteriorating quality of village life. By this they meant that the untouchables (scheduled castes) had become arrogant, the hired hands were acting superior. In addition to all this, Brahmins were concerned about the erosion of their power. Most of these people were furious at Indira Gandhi's government for giving the scheduled castes importance.

It was very disappointing to most villagers that, even though I was concerned for their welfare, I was as helpless as they were. I felt disappointed myself for not being able to do anything substantial for them. Gradually I was accepted for what I was, and the friendly relationship continued. Despite the lower status of women in the village I was considered unique because of my scholarship and was accorded a special status and given special privileges.[5] I was allowed to sit on the same level as men on occasion. I could observe a temple ceremony solely attended by men. A special village Panchayat hearing was conducted for my benefit because I was not allowed to attend the regular meeting from which women are strictly excluded.[6] I learned quite a bit about the relationships between men and women during this hearing.[7]

DIVERGENCE OF VALUE ORIENTATIONS

I spent the first few weeks asking questions of a number of people and taking notes. I tried my best all through my stay in the village just to be a good listener by asking questions and listening to answers intently. In every group I tried to be as inconspicuous as I could, but it was impossible to hide myself completely. There were a few occasions when I had to state my position firmly and stick to it. One of these occurred when I was asked by a young man to lend him my notes to read. He felt he had a right to know what kinds of things I was writing. But I refused and told him that I could not allow him to read papers containing my private thoughts. This made him terribly angry, and he promptly instructed his wife not to talk to me any more.

I also realized that I could not just go on asking questions, but I had to answer many also. Even though I tried to minimize this, there was no way of completely evading the responsiblility. One question that I was asked over and over again was: What do you think of Western women? In the beginning I tried not to say much. But when I was cornered I had to express my true feelings about them. The villagers were shocked to find out that I did not share their evaluation of Western women as being aggressive and immoral.

I believe that a field researcher should not overtly expose or push personal opinions with regard to various issues. But if the situation presents itself one cannot evade such a responsibility. In fact, taking no stand at all could lead to diminished respect and reduce the researcher's effectiveness. I had to reveal my convictions more than once when asked to express my opinions. People came to know that I was strongly opposed to wife abuse when I expressed my shock and dismay at the beating death of a Vokkaliga woman in the village. On one occasion an elderly Brahmin man told how a man taught his wife a good lesson. It seems the wife was getting together with some girl friends after the husband went to work. They would sometimes make some snacks and sweets and have a little party. In short, the wife was having fun without the husband's knowledge and permission. For this the husband punished his wife by burning her knuckles with a big hot iron nail. All the men were laughing loudly when this story was narrated with embellishment. The women were silent as they are not expected to participate in men's conversation. I also sat there grimly without saying anything. Later I found out that the elderly man was angry with me for not laughing at his joke, as he had expected.

In addition, there were several incidents that took place in the village about which I showed my displeasure. One incident took place during a prayer meeting on the Ramanavmi festival day.[8] During this meeting an announcement was made that I would be donating some money to the Rammandir (Temple of Rama). The announcement was made without my knowledge and in my absence. The meeting was attended only by men since women are excluded from such meetings. Several men who had pledged support during this meeting were honored with flowers, betel leaves, and coconut. But, although they wanted my money, they did not want to include me in their meeting (worse than that, they did not even inform me!), nor did they honor me as they honored others. When I expressed my displeasure, I was told that it would have been better if my husband was present at that time. I did not make a big issue out of it, but the very fact that I was displeased surprised them. For them, excluding me from their meeting was right and proper, in keeping with tradition. Their earlier respect for me as one who cherished Hindu tradition must have gone down one notch that day.

Some women also felt that I did not exactly belong with them; they kept me out of their groups and treated me as an inferior while observing pollution rituals. I was often classified along with young children while serving food on special occasions and was not included in their performance of religious rituals. The young children in the community had difficulty in addressing me, an older married person, with respect. Not only was I not behaving like other older married women but I was always . reading books like schoolchildren. They were often chided and corrected by their mothers for addressing me in the singular as they would other children. These incidents—which were neither serious nor frequent—revealed an important point. Just as I could not completely accept them, they could not completely accept me as I was. The ambivalence surfaced now and then and dramatically pointed out the cultural gulf that existed between me and the village people because I did not accept all their tenets of proper behavior. In fact, I was asked by one young man to give one good reason why I deserved respect as a woman when I was not sacrificing anything for my family. He argued that I was always interested in doing the things I liked rather than concentrating on the interests of my husband and children.

RESPONDENTS' POSITION IN THE SOCIAL HIERARCHY

The position in the social hierarchy occupied by the respondents is a very important factor that has to be taken into account while doing field research. The Musali women were strictly under the control of men. I could not obtain any information from them until the men gave permission. Even then the women were generally very reluctant to talk about their relationships with their husbands. I had to devise various strategies like relying on special informants, listening carefully to village gossip, observing the actual relationship carefully whenever possible to get at this kind of information. Every step of the way I had to be very cautious about the kinds of questions I asked, how they were asked, going through proper channels. It was a very delicate task, and I had to be constantly wary lest I commit an irreparable blunder.

The women did not hesitate to cut short our conversation in the middle if their men needed attention, despite the fact that they enjoyed talking to me and felt honored that I considered their opinions important and listened to them intently. I often had to make several trips to find a time when they were free and had to have several sessions before I could get all the information I needed from a given respondent.

When the men realized that I was interested in studying the life of women in the village, my prestige in their eyes suddenly went down. Most of them expressed skepticism about what I could learn about the village by talking with, of all people, women. When it became clear to them that I was collecting data on the life of women in detail, several men were bothered by it. A campaign was launched by them to convince me that women's lives are much better than they seem to be on the surface. I was given several lectures about how Indian womanhood is the best there is. It was made clear to me that the Western way which I had been exposed to and was probably influenced by is degenerate and immoral.

Some men felt self-conscious about the treatment of women in the village and admitted that they were treated as second-class citizens. Their explanation of this situation takes two forms. The first one is that somebody has to be lower and it could as well be women—that is the way it has been, and that has worked best. These people cannot conceptualize a situation where order and stability in the family and larger society can exist without a hierarchical arrangement of people. Their argument is that when the crunch comes someone has to be in charge. Someone has to give orders and others take them. There is a firm conviction that nature does not intend that men and women should be equals. There is also a great deal of concern that if women are treated as equals the joint family system would not work and the older generation would be neglected. Under these circumstances, it is felt, women should be below men, but men should treat them with consideration. These men strongly disapprove of any form of abuse of women.

The other explanation is that women do not deserve any better. Instances were quoted to me which proved that women do not have a sense of justice, honesty, or trustworthiness. Besides, women are ignorant, helpless, and superstitious. Therefore, they should be under the control of men. Men are not to blame if women are ill treated. If they only can prove that they are as good as men then they can be treated as such.

Several Brahmin men in the village considered me a bad influence on their women. Even though most Brahmin women considered my life experiences completely irrelevant, a few of them looked at me with much curiosity and appeared to find in me an example of what women could be. The husbands of these few women felt uncomfortable and regarded our conversations with suspicion. They did not allow their wives to get their pictures taken. Some set limits on what they could talk about. One husband instructed his wife not to talk about sexual aspects of their relationship. Another instructed his wife to make sure that his sister was present when she talked with me. After every session the sister would report the conversations to him. I did not have such trouble in the Vokkaliga community because Vokkaliga women considered me as being very different from themselves and their men had no reason to feel threatened.

In spite of caste divisions, the villagers had a sense of community about the village as a whole. This sentiment was strongest among the Vokkaligas who are the dominant caste in the village. As the power of the Brahmins was eroding gradually in the village there were some members of this caste who did not have a strong sense of loyalty to the village, but many did. The groups that occupied the lower rungs of the social ladder in the village, namely Muslims, scheduled castes, and others, did not feel strongly either. Women felt a sense of loyalty to their families, but not as strongly to the village as a whole. It is important to remember that those who felt this strong sense of loyalty to the village were precisely those who also had the power.

These men with power from both the Vokkaliga and Brahmin communities tried very intently to make sure that I did not write anything damaging to the reputation of the village. I was told that as one belonging to the village, I was like an ambassador and had special responsibilities to the village. I should be loyal to the village and should desist from writing anything that might put Musali in a bad light. I should close my eyes to what I might consider bad and highlight the good aspects. As one man put it, I should have the knack of the swan to separate milk from water and that of the honey bee to extract only the sweet juices. Musali is my *thavaru*,[9] in fact, the whole of India is, since I live in America, and no self-respecting daughter would do anything that might bring a bad name to her *thavaru*. Being a dutiful daughter is so much more important than all the scholarship I might acquire. Yet, the women who provided me with most of my information were excited because I considered it important to write about their life as it actually is.

Chapter III

PATIVRATYA: THE IDEOLOGY

Pativratya has been the dominant ideology governing the lives of women in Hindu society through the years. This androcentric ideology has effectively sustained the patriarchal social structure which gave rise to it in the first place. As Marchak points out, this ideology, just like any other dominant ideology, "provides the ready references, the rules of thumb, the directives to the eyes and ears of its members. It is the glue that holds the institutions together, the medium that allows members of the population to interact, predict events, understand their roles, perform adequately, and—perhaps above all—strive to achieve the kinds of goals most appropriate to the maintenance of any particular social organization" (1975:1). The contents of this ideology becomes clear when we examine what is expected of a Pativrata—a wife who embodies Pativratya. In the words of people of Musali:

> A woman should realize that a man marries to continue his family line by getting sons. He should pay his debt to society, to his ancestors, and thereby ensure the spriritual well-being of his soul. The wife as Pativrata should be his true helpmate by helping him in every possible way to achieve his goals in life. She should never think that she has an existence apart from her husband. His needs should be hers. She should become one with him in every sense of the word.
>
> A Pativrata always eats whatever is left after her husband

has eaten. Even if she was happy in her parent's home she should not think of it in her husband's house. If a woman as much as imagines the good life other couples are having or stops to watch other couples enjoying each other's company, the husband has a right to kill her as she was not completely true to him. Obeying the command of one's husband without question is a mark of virtue and good conduct. She should never be inquisitive. She should never be arrogant. Even a slight indiscretion on the part of the wife towards her husband is a crime and is unbecoming of a Pativrata.

A Pativrata will be happy to die before her husband. Dying in his own hands is an added privilege for her because thereby she surely reaches heaven. A Pativrata burns herself in the funeral pyre of her husband as it is not worth living after her husband's death.

She never expects any concern or consideration from her husband. He does not have to pay attention even when she is in pain. It does not matter whether he is true to her or not. A Pativrata knows that her salvation lies in her devotion to her husband and to him only. She never even looks at another man. She believes *Pati pratyaksha devatha* (Husband is the living God).

A true Pativrata has extraordinary powers which she accumulates by doing austere services to her husband. She can, for example, turn stone into food, turn gods into children, and bring dead husbands back to life—just as the wives of great sages did. She should listen to stories of great Pativratas in her spare time so that she will be inspired by them.

This ideology is based on certain assumptions and beliefs regarding the nature of men and women and their proper interrelationship. People have a strong opinion that there is a basic difference in the natures of men and women. Men are ritually pure, physically strong, and emotionally mature; women, on the other hand, are ritually pollutable, physically weak, and lack strong willpower.

Women are also thought of as having a corrupting influence on men. I was quoted many wise sayings and excerpts from songs to prove that the woman is one of the important impediments preventing a man's smooth spiritual journey. The impediment does not arise because of anything a woman does directly; her sheer presence has a corrupting influence on man's spiritual nature. Sex is something that veers a man away from his path toward spiritual enlightenment; woman is the personification of sex and therefore a temptation to man. Sarvajna, the saint, writes: "Where are the men that can look at women, ripe fruits or gold and not desire them?" A woman can minimize this temptation by dressing with modesty and keeping away from the presence of men as much as possible.

Women are believed to be unscrupulous and to dominate men, given a chance. They have no sense of proportion, because *Stree buddhi pralayanthakaha* (Woman's intellect is destructive). Besides, as the saying goes, *Olidare nari munidare mari* (A woman's behavior is unpredictable). Men are cautioned not to rely on a woman's assessment of situations and not to get into a quarrel with anyone on the basis of a woman's words. Men should always keep a social distance so that a woman understands her place. It is strongly believed that a woman should not be given power. I was given the example of Indira Gandhi and told, "Look how destructive a woman's intelligence can be!" When I asked how come so many men in power have created so much havoc over the centuries, I was told that "there is always reason for such actions on the part of men. Only rarely one finds a stupid man in power who makes mistakes. But, women have an evil influence on things if they get into positions of power. It is their nature to be destructive." That is why *Hengasu gandana neralinalli balabeku* (A woman should always live in her husband's shadow).

The belief is strong that men should lead and women follow. That it is the way God intended it to be:

> To run things smoothly someone has to give orders and others have to follow it. Nature has intended that men give orders and women follow. Otherwise men would be bearing children and women would have been stronger.

There is a strong conviction of the natural order of things and that such an order should not be tampered with. The frequency of famines, drought, floods, diseases, and wars can only be attributed to the declining morality resulting from tampering with the natural order. The only way to stop this decline is for each person to know his or her place in the natural order and behave accordingly.

It is assumed that a woman cannot protect herself because she is physically weak and has weak willpower. Her body is structured in such a way that if she is attacked the result is the defilement of her person and she becomes like a *Nayi muttida madake* (earthen pot touched by a dog). The only way you can purify that pot is by throwing it into burning fire. So it is for a woman. Such defilement would destroy the whole social fabric, and nothing would remain. Almost everyone in the village is vehemently against giving freedom to women since the consequence will be nothing short of disaster. The purity of her body is of paramount importance, and it is the man's repsonsibility to protect the woman and keep her body ritually pure. So much is at stake, she should be protected even at the expense of her personal freedom and autonomy.

Most villagers—men and women—agree with what one man told me:

> Arranged marriage is the best type of marriage. No one can risk marrying a woman that was running around with other men as there is no guarantee that her body is still unpolluted. What will happen to your *Vamsha* [family tree] if you marry and have children with such a woman? One should only marry a virgin who is pure and then have children. That is the only way a man can be sure of having proper children to perpetuate his sacred family tree. Otherwise he will be destroying it by polluting it. There is nothing more unholy than a son born of a polluted woman giving oblations to his ancestors. Instead of doing that one can as well kill everyone in the family and destroy the family tree.

It logically follows that a woman can marry one and only one husband, and have children only by him. She should always be careful to preserve her purity by maintaining strict marital fidelity. A woman who is untrue to her husband deserves to die. Marriage is a sacred union, and a woman should realize that her body and soul belong to her husband.

In the same breath, I was told that women as mothers deserve to be respected. Besides, a mother's love and the kind of nurturance she gives is something very precious and special. It is instructive to note how the observation made by Douglas (1975:60–62) fits in with the opinions expressed by the people of Musali. She points out that, in a society where male supremacy is considered to be the right state of affairs but women are still believed to have qualities that entitle them to special treatment, the pollution beliefs are used to legitimize the superiority of men. Her arguments are certainly applicable in this context. There is a firm conviction that male supremacy is the right state of affairs, and there definitely is a good deal of ambivalence in conceptualization of a woman's nature. She is believed to be deserving of respect as a mother but as a person she cannot be trusted or relied upon.

The opinions expressed by the people of Musali are in no way unique but have a firm basis in Hindu thought where the differential nature of men and women and the proper relationship between them is clearly laid out. There is a strong belief in the dualistic conception of woman's nature (Buhler 1886; Jacobson and Wadley 1977:113–34). She is believed to have both good and bad aspects in her.[1] The bad aspect can erupt when a woman is displeased and the good aspect when she is happy and contented. Every attempt is made to suppress and neutralize the bad aspect and create conditions for manifestation of the good aspect. Manu's discussion of the proper position of women clearly reveals this belief. He wrote consistently that a woman should always be under the care and direction of men. She should always be respected as a mother. Her material needs and comforts should be taken care of so that she will have no occasion to feel bad (Buhler 1886: Ch. V, 148, Ch. IX, 1–17).

Male and female principles are different, but they need to come together to create and sustain life. The male principle represents consciousness (*Vijnana*) whereas the female principle is energy (*Shakti*). Several systems of Hindu philosophy, notably Sankhya-Yoga and Tantric philosophy, elaborate on the significant differences between these two principles as well as their essential unity when it comes to the creation and sustanance of life (Radhakrishnan and Moore 1957; Dasgupta 1963; Agrawala 1963). In addition, the female is closer to nature because of her role in the reproductive process; she provides the soil to nurture the seed provided by the male.[2] Since seed is more important than soil and undefined energy lacks direction, it is considered imperative that man—the provider of seed and direction—should be in control. Also a woman's body is susceptible to pollution. Sexual intercourse results in such pollution; therefore, a woman's sexuality needs to be controlled. Only a virgin is fit to bear proper sons, and therefore virginity at the time of marriage is mandatory for a woman. After marriage, the husband should protect his wife's honor so that she remains true to him and continues to be fit to bear his sons.

The belief that a woman is impulsive by nature and therefore should be under the direction of men is reflected in the way mother goddesses are treated. The female goddesses are considered benevolent when accompanied by male gods, but when alone they are considered impulsive and unpredictable (Babb 1975:223–26). Manu justifies the subjugation of women precisely on the basis of the differential nature and potential of men and women (Buhler 1886:Ch. IX, V. 1–17).

The conception of the merging of male and female principles under the control of the male is expressed in the names of gods who create, sustain, and destroy life—Parvathi Parameshwara, and Laxmi Narayana. The first part of the name is female and the second, male. The female is conceptualized as residing in the male. According to the story of Mahisha (the buffalo demon), Durga-Kali (personification of *Shakti*) was produced from the radiant flames that issued from the mouth of Shiva to kill Mahisha.[3]

The method of worship of female deities also reveals the interdependence of male and female principles. Once a year in the village of Musali (more often if the village is going through an unusual hardship like the outbreak of epidemics or drought), the village goddess is worshipped in an elaborate manner by the Brahmin community.[4] The ceremony begins by invoking the presence of the male god Ishwara, the husband of the mother goddess Parvati, and praying that he incorporate the deity within him. Then the two together are worshipped with an elaborate ritual, including the chanting of hymns and the offering of flowers, incense, and food. The goddess will do the job of protecting the village but Ishwara must show her the way. I was told by the priests that the goddess will not behave impulsively but in a predictable manner once such worship is performed.

The belief that female principle is imbedded in the male also explains the attitude and behavior towards widows. People do not see any reason for mourning the death of a woman because as long as her husband is alive she continues to be part of him. It is only her mortal body that is dead, and if she has been a true Pativrata she has found her salvation. But, on the other hand, when the husband dies, she is also dead as she is a part of him. Even though her mortal body is alive the spirit is gone. The custom of *sati*[5] was justified on this basis. It was argued that once the real essence of the person is gone there is no use to keep the mortal body alive. When stringent laws were passed to prevent *sati*, to avoid any kind of pollution to the body which would endanger the fate of the spirit the practice of purification of widows took its place. The widow was supposed to live only to atone for her sins and always had to be faithful to the memory of her husband.

These views about women are similar in spirit to the position taken about a woman's ability to achieve in different fields of endeavor. Her ability is never questioned, but the wisdom of striving for achievement is. How the accumulated knowledge and cultivated talent will be used by a woman without man's direction is considered problematic. The nagging fear always is that a woman might forget her true nature because of her acquired knowledge and skills, the result of which would be nothing less than disaster.[6] The people of Musali are very afraid of the world plunging into chaos if women were to gain too much freedom.

To maintain the purity of the female body fit for reproduction a woman has to be kept under the control of men. But as giver of life and nurturer of children she is revered. As Ranganathananda writes: "This symbol of self-effacing love has revealed to the Hindu mind the presence of a divine reality within, over and above the personality of the visible mother. To the Hindu, God is the mother of all creation. A nation that has educated itself to look upon God as mother has learned to invest its view of woman with the utmost tenderness and reverence. The culture of the Hindu trains him to look upon all women, nay, to look upon the female of all species, as forms of the one Divine Mother. The mother is more worthy of reverence than father or teacher according to our scriptures . . ." (Allen and Mukherjee 1982:10).

But this does not mean that a woman can feel a sense of power and use it to her own advantage. To cite Ranganathananda again:

> And what constitutes this abundant glory in the mother is her self-effacing love and compassion, which, to the Hindu, is a mark of high spirituality and true culture ... it is this vision that India has always held out before her women and which her daughters have passionately struggled to realise in their lives. Even the apparent failings of her women proceed largely from that passion. The practice of *suttee* [*sati*], for example, proceeds from loyalty to the ideal of chastity which found itself threatened in a chaotic society.
>
> The ideals of chastity and purity, unselfishness and service, simplicity and modesty, have been pursued by our women, drawn by that vision of innate divinity. The Indian woman cannot jump out of this inheritance of hers. Warned Swami Vivekenada more than fifty-six years ago, "Any attempt to modernise our women, if it tries to take our women away from the ideal of Sita,[7] is immediately a failure, as we see every day. The women of India must grow and develop in the footprints of Sita, and that is the only way" (Ibid.).

Hence, even though motherhood in principle is revered and worshipped, to be deserving of it a woman has to abide by the ideology of Pativratya. The Epics and Puranas elaborate this ideology, and women are fed on this in stong doses over and over again. As Altekar points out, even though women were denied opportunity to study the Vedas and the Upanishads, the practical guidance to their lives was provided through popular literature (1956:25). The Epics and the Puranas are imparted to women generation after generation in the form of storytelling (*harikathas*) or in motion pictures depicting the lives of gods and goddesses personifying this ideology. The famous Pativratas who figure prominently are Ahalya, Draupadi, Tara, Sita, and Mandodari.[8] The spirit of this ideology is embedded in any discussion of Indian womanhood. In the popular consciousness the image of Sita, the famous epic heroine of Ramayana, reigns supreme. Each woman is taught to know her true nature as possessor of a pollutable body and an impulsive mind but with a potential to be a nurturer. She should understand that her life goal is to be of service to her husband and cater to his every need, including being a good mother to his children. She should develop the proper disposition to achieve these goals because that is where her salvation lies. Achievement of salvation by escaping from the cycle of rebirth of course is everyone's ultimate life goal. Women can achieve this by being Pativratas.

As Guy Rocher points out, this ideology has become to the Hindus a system of ideas and judgments, which are explicit and generally organized; which serve to describe, explain, interpret or justify the situation of a group or collectivity; and which, largely on the basis of values, suggest a precise orientation to the historical action of this group or collectivity (1972:103).

Difference in caste background does not matter much since the ideology with its complex set of ideas directs women to maintain male authority in all castes. The influence of the ideology is all-pervasive, and a Pativrata in any caste tries her best to live in the shadow of her husband and does her utmost to discharge her wifely duties. Owing to variation in life-styles the caste duties differ in different castes. But the continuing thread of argument is that women embody energy which is to be used by men for their own benefit. As Allen and Mukherjee write,

> For the village men, that is, the men of the world, women were substantively, though variously, valued; by the Brahmins as pure indices of high status, by the Kshatriya and Vaisya as fertile producers of progeny, and by the Śudra as sources of material and sensuous satisfaction. For the forest-dwelling seeker after *moksha*, that is, for this world renouncer who has removed himself from the phenomenal world of social process, women were negatively viewed as without value. Controlling women, dominating them, and using them for own benefit by the men is considered proper and legitimate in all castes (1982:16).

The belief that women exist for the comfort of men is quite widespread in the village. That they should be taken care of in terms of providing the material needs and comforts that a husband is capable of is also widely held. It is considered right and proper for the husbands to use wives as they see fit to achieve the goals they set for themselves.

The ideology is interpreted as divinely ordained for the good of humanity. When confronted with examples of inhuman treatment of women, ad hoc explanations are given, thereby dismissing the incidents as trivial exceptions due to situational exigencies and particular personal failures.

Women are exhorted to cultivate the noble qualities like gentleness, docility, and selflessness. Literary writers like Tagore express the opinion that the whole life plan is to tame the unbridled energy of women and turn it to the service of mankind (Sengupta 1974:41). Vivekanada, a respected philosopher and saint, expresses similar ideas when he writes that the noble qualities of womanhood which are soothing to the eye and comforting to the soul should never be abandoned and should be cultivated. Women are advised, and girls are instructed, to have a smiling face even in adversity and never to heave a sigh of discontent (1962–70: Vol. VIII, 198; Vol. V, 231; Vol. VI, 145–50).

This ideology is presented to the woman as something that is natural and eternal. No attempt is made to explain, but it is ascertained as self-evident truth. The presentation is done with an emotional fervor and religious conviction that prevent any questioning of its validity. The objective always is to "help" women develop the conviction that the state of affairs they are confronted with is right, proper, necessary, and desirable.

The end result is, as Daly points out: "The belief system becomes hardened and objectified, seeming to have an unchangeable, independent existence and validity of its own. It resists social change that would rob it of its plausibility" (1973:13).

Chapter IV

WOMEN'S LIVES WITHIN THE FAMILY STRUCTURE

The androcentric ideology of Pativratya is built into the patriarchal social structure prevalent in the village of Musali. Definite limits are set in terms of available opportunities in such a way that women are directed towards becoming dependent on men economically. Interpersonal relationships are structured to maintain hierarchical relationships between the sexes, with men in the higher position, and division of labor along sex lines is in effect, with a stigma attached to women's work. Since the structures are rigidly set without viable alternate options, women cannot do anything but conform and accept the secondary position accorded them. Deviant behavior is dealt with promptly, formally and informally, thereby bringing people back in line with expected behavior.

To understand the structure of interpersonal relationships in Musali one has to study the family. Women do not participate in the political arena, and only a very negligible number of them (one Brahmin and three Vokkaliga women) work for wages outside the home or, being widows, are involved in commercial activities on their own.

THE FAMILY

Among both Brahmins and Vokkaligas, the family structure is patriarchal, patrilineage is recognized, and the residential pattern is patrilocal. Marriages are arranged. The ideal family type is the joint family. All respondents either had lived or were still living in such context. Property is inherited by and transmitted through male heirs. The name children take is that of the father. The wife ceases to be a member of her family of birth and becomes a member of her husband's family. She occupies a marginal status in this family until she has children, at which time she is fully integrated into the family. Financial decisions are generally made by the husband. However, a wife may be consulted if her husband so chooses. Decisions regarding running of the household are generally made jointly.

Ever since Independence in 1947, laws have been passed to make women equal to men as persons, entitling them to an equal share in inheritance of property, but these laws have not changed the women's status. In Musali only a handful (three women) have heard of these laws but none of them knows what it is all about and how it affects them. Luschinsky (1963) reports the same finding in her study done in North India.

The family structure has remained almost the same in the last twenty years except that some joint families have broken up and the power of the mother-in-law over daughter-in-law is reduced somewhat. In the past the joint family used to consist of parents, sons, their wives, and their children. Now one often finds parents, their unmarried children, one son, and his family. In Musali, there used to be some joint families with several brothers living under one roof, sharing property jointly. Now there are only two cases where two or more brothers are living together with their families. And, as in the past, if a man has one or more un-married brothers, sisters, or widowed parents, these usually live with him. There are some instances where even a widowed mother is made to live by herself. A greater proportion of families tends to be nuclear as compared to the past. Epstein (1973:200–6) also observes a gradual in-crease in the proportion of nuclear to joint families in her study of a Karnataka village.

Among the women of the village, only four married into another family in the same village. All other women come originally from neigh-boring villages and a few from small towns. The custom in this village is somewhat different from that of North India, where the brides invar-iably come from a different village (Wiser and Wiser 1971:262; Minturn and Hitchcock 1966:27; Carstairs 1961:45).

Marriages are arranged, and subcaste endogamy is scrupulously followed. Husbands are always older than wives, and the disparity might range from three to fifty years, but a five-to-six year age difference is most common. Also, husbands are generally taller in stature than wives and are better educated.

Arranging a marriage is an art and needs a certain amount of ex-pertise. Usually older men and women play an important role in this because they have experience and the time. Arranging a marriage can take anywhere from six months to three or more years.[1]

The dowry system is still prevalent among the Brahmins. The father of the bride also has to pay for the marriage expenses, and the marriage generally takes place in the the bride's house. In this village, among the Vokkaligas bride price was in vogue about twenty years ago, but the dowry system is practiced at the present time by most families even though the size of the dowry is never as big as it is among Brahmins. Srinivas (1976:154) in his study of Rampura, a village in Karnataka, reports that the system of bride price is prevalent among the Vokkaligas. The data for his study were collected in 1948. We do not know whether the system has changed in recent years there also.

Physical strength plays an important role in the selection of the proper mate for a woman, as farming and village life in general require it. Strong men are admired and respected and are considered as ideal mates. Among the Vokkaligas, strength and stamina are looked for even among women. In negotiating marriages, a frail woman who tends to get sick often is avoided. However, this criterion of physical strength is not very important for a woman among Brahmins, as she is not in general expected to work in the fields.

When she gets married, woman becomes by definition part of her husband or *Ardhangi*, thereby losing her separate identity. While making out invitations for celebrations like weddings, the custom is to write *Srimati* (Mrs.) and *Sri* (Mr.) after which the husband's name is written. The family itself is known by the man's name. While listing the names of well-wishers in a wedding card, only men's names appear or they have the prefix *Srimati* attached to it. This is true even in cases where the person who is getting married is the woman's brother. A woman cannot participate in any religious activity on her own; everything must be done in the name of her husband. This was driven home to me very clearly in the village when I wanted a prayer service to the deity performed in my name, using it as a pretext to distribute sweets to the villagers as an expression of my gratitude. The service could only be performed through my husband, not on my own.

Ideally, when the bride comes to her new home, she should be welcomed, accepted, and cherished. She is the *Lakshmi* (goddess of wealth) that has come to bless the home. She has come to the new home leaving all her loved ones who were near and dear to her. It is said in the sacred books that the gods feel satisfied when a woman is made to feel happy in her new home. If she is made to feel sad, bad luck will befall the family.

The reality of the situation is often more complex than what is ideally expected. For the members of the family, accepting a stranger in their midst as part of the family, especially when she occupies a privileged position with the son of the household, is a very difficult task. In spite of the ideals, the bride may face hostility. The adjustment is relatively smooth when efforts are made by both sides and there is a genuine willingness on the part of both the parties to achieve amity. Sometimes it is just a matter of time. At others, the personalities clash, and adjustments are hard to make.

The patriarchal nature of the family, patrilineage, and partilocality create structural conditions which make the status of the woman a marginal one. Karve (1963) clearly delineates the marginal position women occupy in the kinship structure. Her observations are very similar to the ones made in this study. This is especially true regarding a woman's lack of the right to inherit property. A woman's position is one of economic dependence and is subject to the vagaries of chance. She has to rely upon the whims and fancies of men and depend upon their good will. A woman's life is not entirely sad in a situation where her husband is concerned about her welfare. If the people in the husband's family are conscientious, they will take pity on her and treat her with kindness. But, if they are people with no scruples, then, with no place to go and no one to appeal to, a woman has to accept whatever comes as her destiny.

Although there is often much friction in the joint family situation, generally some kind of accommodation is worked out. One such accommodation consists in the complete acceptance of the authority structure in the family by the daughter-in-law. She remains meek and submissive, and the mother-in-law rules the family. If she is a good worker and bears sons, she is accepted as a member of the family even though in a low status. Usually in such cases the son is controlled by his parents and has low status in the family also, though not so low as his wife's.

A typical example of such an accommodation in Musali is Rajayya's (Satya's father) family (see Appendix A, Case History 16). The mother-in-law Kamalamma has a very strong personality and is very close to her son Satya. Her daughter-in-law Seema is extremely docile and meek even after living in the family for five years and bearing a daughter. She does most of the work in the household, yet has no say in any decision making. I asked some neighbors if the situation would improve if Seema had a son. The neighbors were very skeptical about this possibility since Satya and his mother are so very close and the mother is strong.

In cases where the daughter-in-law refuses to be meek and submissive, the family might still remain intact, but the power structure in the family is altered. Usually in such cases the father is not alive, and the son is the dominant person. The mother is relegated to an inferior status as she is in a very poor bargaining position. She will accept such an arrangement and will start to lead her life in a marginal position, not getting herself involved in any of the goings-on in the family.

Rangappa's family is a typical example of such an accommodation. Basamma has been married to Rangappa for two years now and has a son (see Appendix A, Case History 39). In that short time she has firmly established herself in her husband's family by isolating her widowed mother-in-law. The old woman has no choice but to toe the line Basamma draws. The son is close to his wife and does not want to antagonize her.

When the personalities of the mother-in-law and daughter-in-law clash and neither gives in, the family might break up, whereby the son will set up a house of his own, taking a share of the parental property. This solution is looked down upon, and such daughters-in-law are thought of as home wreckers. But it happens nevertheless. Such instances generally arise when there develops a close affinity between husband and wife, or there are several sons and a sibling rivalry develops in the family, prompting one son to get out of the parental household.

In the case of Krishnappa's family, his wife Vanajamma and daughter-in-law Janaki could not get along at all (see Appendix A, Case History 15). Besides, his son Venku always had disagreements with his four brothers, especially with Prabhu, who is next to him. This situation led to the breakup of the family which is still lamented by Vanajamma who blames her daughter-in-law every chance she gets.

Usually, when parents die, the married sons set up households of their own, and the property is divided among them. In the nuclear family context, the newly married couple develops an amicable relationship over time with relative ease as there are no other persons to interfere. In many marriages mutual trust and a kind of companionship develop within the hierarchical context. The wife scrupulously follows all the deference customs. The husband has no reason to question her loyalty and subservience. She serves him well in bed and in the kitchen. He gradually starts to talk to her about various things when he feels like it. The wife never questions her husband's behavior. But the husband being satisfied with her remains loyal to her and slowly starts to confide in her. The wife feels flattered when this happens and expresses her gratitude. In essence, the wife develops and sustains a negative and low self-image, idealizes her husband, and holds him in high regard, identifying her interests with his. In the words of an old man in Musali, she is a servant when doing his work, she gives counsel like a minister, she is forgiving as the earth herself, she is like a prostitute in bed, and so on. Besides, she is always there when he needs her but never bothers him or complains about her own welfare. The husband cherishes such a wife and takes care of her, making sure she has all the material comforts he is capable of providing. This type of affable marriage is ideal in the Indian context.

Kapur (1970:432–33) in her study of women and family adjustment writes that even in urban areas, only those marriages are well adjusted where women play traditional roles; in those families in which women question the legitimacy of such a relationship the marriage tends to be on a shaky ground.

Once an amicable relationship is developed, the wife may suggest and remind her husband of various things to be done. She has to manage the household, so she can ask for things needed to run the house. She is expected to run the house befitting the status of her husband and mindful of family tradition. To get her own way, she may use feminine wiles like crying, fasting, and gradually learning to recognize her husband's idiosyncrasies and developing strategies to manipulate him.

DEFERENCE CUSTOMS

It was 1:00 in the afternoon. Saroja was ready at the door with water in a clean shining brass vessel and a towel, as her husband Ramu came home from work. She poured water as he washed his hands, face, and feet and then handed the towel to him to dry himself. She gave him a glass of water to drink as Ramu walked into the kitchen where the place was set for the family midday meal. Saroja had set the mats on the floor, plates and glasses filled with water for her in-laws, her three children, and her husband. The father-in-law sat at the head of the line, Ramu next to him. Her two sons sat next to their father. In the opposite line, her mother-in-law sat with her granddaughter.[2]

Saroja then served food, waiting attentively on everyone. The in-laws and the husband were engaged in conversation, and the children were talking among themselves.

Saroja had not said a single word so far. When Ramu asked her if anyone came to call on him when he was away, she said yes, there was someone but he did not leave his name. She said all this in a barely audible voice.

After eveyone was finished Saroja cleared the place and sat for her meal and served herself whatever was left. While the other members of the family relaxed in the veranda she cleaned the kitchen and all the dishes. The men left for work after about an hour, and the mother-in-law went next door to chat. Only then did Saroja come out to the verandah and sit down on a mat, her legs stretched out. The husband returned home unexpectedly as he had forgotten to take his hand towel, and Saroja stood up in a hurry in embarrassment and went to the inner chamber. She then came out feeling apologetic for sitting stretched out on the mat. She was thankful that her mother-in-law had not seen her. Her mother-in-law came in soon after, as she was engaged in cleaning the rice and getting things ready for the evening meal and next morning's breakfast. Saroja talked with her mother-in-law only when the latter wanted to discuss the breakfast. Her answer was again in a low voice. After a while her mother-in-law left for the fields to take care of the cattle.

Much the same routine was followed at night, and Saroja waited until everyone was in bed before she went to bed herself. She was glad to finally retire so that she may catch as much sleep as possible because she knew she had to get up in the morning before everyone else to start the day and get everything ready for her family by the time they woke up.

This account depicting Saroja's day is an illustration of the typical style of interpersonal relationship within a Vokkaliga family. The same type of behavior is evident among Brahmins also except for some differences in detail due to variation in life-style. For example, if there is a mother-in-law in the house she usually serves the meal, and the daughter-in-law acts as apprentice. This is because the older Brahmin woman is very concerned about ritual pollution and does not let her daughter-in-law touch the food. The mother-in-law and daughter-in-law eat after the men and children have finished. The daughter-in-law does everything that does not involve touching cooked food.

Deference customs are expected to be followed strictly by the women of both castes in their relationship with their husbands. The wife is expected to eat only after her husband eats, sleep only after he sleeps, walk behind him, sit below him, never sit when he is standing, and speak only when spoken to. She must also adhere to the specified linguistic style while talking with her husband. The hierarchical structure of interrelationship is built into the language. She refers to him only in the plural like *avaru* (they, not he) whereas he can use singular like *neenu* (you, singular) or *avalu* (she). She never addresses him by name; only equals or superiors can do this. To reinforce such behavior there is a strong belief that if a wife utters her husband's name his longevity will be diminished—which is the most dreaded event. She never addresses him directly and while talking to others refers to him as *namma yajamanaru* (my lord) or *avaru* (they). He refers to her as *nammake* (she who is mine) or *nanna ardhangi* (one who shares half of my being).

If she needs to ask him to bring something from the market, she will say it indirectly—*Uppu bekagithu* (Salt is needed) or *Aushadhi bekagithu* (Medicine is needed). She never says *Uppu tha* (Bring salt) or *Aushadhi tha* (Bring medicine). The husband is informed about what needs to be done, and he will decide what to do and whether to do it. Wiser and Wiser (1971:262; Carstairs 1961:66) observe a similar style of behavior on the part of younger women in their relationship with their husbands and all the elders in the family.

An older woman is also expected to be deferential towards men, but in general this requirement is strictly observed only when a man is older than the woman. It is the younger woman who is expected to follow the rules most scrupulously. Among Brahmins even older women follow this one since it is considered a sign of good breeding. Older Vokkaliga women on the other hand ignore such requirements most of the time.

A woman is responsible for serving food to all members of the family before she herself eats. This custom is relaxed in some families, where there are several women. In such cases, one woman serves, and all others eat together. There is always sex segregation in the seating arrangement while eating, and men are always served each item before women even if they are all sitting together to eat. This custom is so rigorously followed that even in cases where the sweets and other dishes are served to devotees after the worship and offering to the god, men must be served first. I observed this practice when I arranged for a service conducted to the god in my husband's name. Even though it is considered an honor to serve the *Prasada* (offering) first to the devotee who had the service conducted and paid for it, exceptions are made in cases where women pay. Because she has to have the service done through her husband, she is automatically ineligible to take the position of the devotee who had the services conducted. By definition, she cannot have the services done on her own. Therefore, even if she pays for it, she is served along with the other women after all the men are served. This is customary in every gathering of men and women during any function or ceremony.

There is a kitchen in one corner of the house and the bathroom in another, both separated from the living quarters. The latrine is invariably located some distance from the house, in the corner of the backyard garden, for use by women and girls. Men and boys use the outdoors, fields and gardens, to answer their nature's call.

The interior design of the house is such that there usually are at least two halls, one of which generally is lower than the other, referred as *melina hajara* (top hall) and *kelagina hajara* (bottom hall). During times of harvest the produce is kept in these halls before it is cured and stored or sold. Men and women sleep in different halls, with men and boys invariably in the *melina hajara*. The seating arrangement during various gatherings reflects the gender hierarchy—with only the men seated in the *melina hajara*. The same rule is also followed for seating while serving food during various functions. The segregation of sexes is even more pronounced in parts of North India where women are required to restrict their movements to the inner courtyard (Wiser and Wiser 1971:262; Carstairs 1961:66).

Finer pieces of linen and a greater share of water for the bath (if there is a shortage) go to the men. If there is a shortage of curds or *ghee* (clarified butter) or whatever, the men and boys get their share first, and if anything is left, women and girls get it. Exceptions are made for girls who are babies or if women are pregnant or have given birth recently.

Both men and women are very concerned to establish that the men in the family are smarter than the women. In most instances it is in fact so but wherever it is not the case (for reasons such as a man being shy, unwell, or having some problems), both take a lot of trouble and go to any length to convince themselves and others that it is so. This point is made especially in front of outsiders. For example, a woman may give her ideas to her husband in private and encourage him to present it in front of spectators as his own. Women are not supposed to talk in front of others and even though it is in fact the woman who made the decision, it is projected as being made by the man. This is considered as perfectly legitimate to protect the prestige of the family and its members. Neither the husband wants to look henpecked nor the wife bossy. It is in the interest of both to keep this family secret. Otherwise both will become victims of gossip and character assassination.

Physical strength plays an important role in intersex relationships. Men are very conscious of their superior physical strength and like to keep women constantly aware of this fact. As there is general consensus that this is one of the deference-entitling qualities, they think it is legitimate to use it periodically to keep women under control.[3] This show of physical strength has been carried to such extremes that women have been killed. During my stay in Musali, two women were said to have been killed by their husbands, but the incidents were hushed up with the help of leaders in the village. Relatives of these women (brothers, uncles, etc.) were bribed to keep quiet. One woman was believed to have disobeyed her husband and bought some bangles. This was the "final straw," as the woman had often overstepped her boundaries. Besides, the man was known to have a quick temper. The second woman was rumored to have been killed because of in-law problems in the joint family. The mother-in-law and daughter-in-law never got along well, and the son was on the side of his mother.

Instead of causing regret, such incidents have been used by other men in the village to their advantage. They told their own wives that if a woman misbehaves she would endure the same fate as these dead women. And these incidents have helped to keep the women in line. What is more ironic is that the husbands of the dead women remarried almost immediately.

There is no doubt that a certain amount of respect is shown to women in both communities. Women are important, even indispensable for fulfillment of many aspects of man's life, but a given wife can be replaced by another who can fulfill similar obligations. In other words, even though women in general are considered indispensable, a particular woman is not. In the case of the mother, however, the argument is different: a mother's love is the most precious thing in the world and there is absolutely no substitute for it.

To earn respect and consideration a woman has to behave in the prescribed manner and know her place. She should accept that her role in life is to be a good wife and mother, and she should find her own salvation in doing her duty. She can indulge herself if the situation permits, by having more jewelry or *sarees*, but she should always know that her needs come last.

HUSBAND-WIFE VS. MOTHER-SON RELATIONSHIP

Even though in both relationships the woman is solicitous, nurturing, and concerned, there is a very important difference in the basic principles of the relations between a husband and a wife and a mother and a son. In the latter relation, the norm of reciprocity is operative. The mother carries the son in her womb, goes through childbirth, nurtures him, and brings him up into a young man, all the time making many personal sacrifices. A mother is very particular about pointing these things out to her son. The son has a duty to repay this kindness by taking care of his mother when she is old and meanwhile showing gratitude and respect for everything she did for him. Love, respect, and reverence are due to her as his life giver. For a son, mother is more sacred than father and the respect due to a mother far exceeds that which is due to a father.

Almost always the love of the mother is reciprocated by the son. Even when the son is an adult, one can see him indulged in affectionate conversation with his mother. Nevertheless, as most mothers told me with tears in their eyes, sons become distant as they grow older. "You lose them," one woman told me, "just as you have lost everyone you loved and cherished (namely, parents, brothers)." As they become young men, the sons would rather be seen with men than with or among women. The mothers cherish the time when their sons were young and used to sit on their laps or next to them, bringing comfort to their distraught lives. Even though the mothers feel bad when their sons grow away from them, the feelings are worse when they see them with their own wives. In Musali, the hostility between mother-in-law and daughter-in-law was in most cases very intense, although the sons were not very close to their wives. The very fact that this new woman had a special place in her son's life was most painful for the mother to bear. According to Ross (1961:282–84), who studied the implications of the structural change of families from joint to nuclear in the urban setting, the husband-wife tie is probably becoming somewhat closer than the mother-son tie.

The prevailing belief among village women that girls brought up in the urban environment tend to pull the sons away from the mother seems to have some support. A more detailed and systematic study is required to test the proposition. In any case, in the village context, the mother-son bond appears to be quite strong.

One incident that I observed succinctly summarizes the kinds of conflicts faced by the son in his relationship to his mother. Venki was always particular about pointing out to Raju, her forty-year-old son, the kind of sacrifices she made to bring him up, especially after the death of his father when he was only a child (see Appendix A, Case History 17). She used to get furious if her son bought a *saree* for his wife without bringing one for her at the same time. In addition, she used to demand that her son punish her grandchildren whenever they disobeyed her and also his wife Seethu if she did not pay proper respect. If Raju did not do everything she asked of him right away, she used to fast, cry, and tell everyone how a mother sacrifices everything for her son but the son discards her the minute he has his own family. Raju, unable to withstand these pressures, usually did whatever his mother asked of him. But once in exasperation he asked a friend of his mother to show him a way to cope with so many and often so unreasonable demands. The friend replied that there was not much anyone else could do. Raju would have to find his own way of coping as there was no escape from a relationship that is irrevokeable. In one Vokkaliga family Ramu, the son, had become a habitual drinker and was spending as little time as possible at home since he could not stand the pressure put on him by his mother Sathamma (see Appendix A, Case History 17). Saroja, his wife, was known to get severe beatings if she said anything about his drinking habits. Not all mothers are like this, but they often do pose problems to their sons and put their conjugal relationships in jeopardy.

The relationship between husband and wife is not necessarily a reciprocal relationship. A Pativrata never expects anything from her husband but serves him with all her heart and soul. She never asks him for anything, since the meaning of Pativratya is lost if a wife expects the least bit from her husband.

Even though it is generally expected that the husband should take care of his wife's material needs and comforts, it is also clearly understood that the wife cannot demand it as a matter of right. It is up to the man to make the decision. She should only do her duty and hope for the best. In cases where he is not satisfied with her, for example, if she does not bear sons or she is not good in bed, he can discard her and marry again.[4] There have been three such cases in Musali (two Vokkaliga, one Brahmin) where everyone felt that the man was justified. But the same privileges are not available for a woman: for her marriage is for life.[5]

Husbands are always very particular about maintaining the proper authority relationship with their wives. It is considered necessary to maintain a clear social distance lest his authority erode. This is considered especially important in the first few years of marriage during which time the ground rules for a proper relationship are set. Joking and laughing with a wife are bad—they might give her an impression that she is close to him in status. Physical abuse in moderate quantities is considered necessary if the wife tends to domineer. It is better that she learn right away who is boss or else it will be difficult in the future. Therefore, the focus in husband-wife relationships is not the development of companionship but of hierarchy. Men are convinced that women use their feminine wiles and erode their authority and they should therefore always be on guard. It is true that some women use subtle strategies to get their own way. They maneuver and manipulate. All of this is done within the structural limits. For example, no woman openly questions the authority of her husband. She might manipulate him to get rid of his mother whom she might dislike, or convince him to buy her *sarees* and jewelry. In all other areas her reputation is as much at stake as his own. She certainly does not want to be the butt of ridicule by becoming bossy.

This concern about being considered bossy is sometimes taken to extremes. The case of Latha illustrates this point (see Appendix A, Case History 19). She was very disappointed that her husband was not aggressive enough to stand up and fight for his rights. Because of his indecision the family had lost a plot of land to neighbors who claimed it as their own. Despite her pleadings, he refused even to take the dispute to the Panchayat. When I asked Latha why she herself did not speak up in view of the fact that the neighbor's wife also was involved in the takeover of the land, her answer was that her neighbor Gowri had already earned the reputation as a bossy woman and therefore had nothing to lose by getting involved directly. The whole village made fun of Gowri and her husband, and therefore they had difficulty in getting their daughter married. Latha dreaded the same type of thing happening to her.

As the emphasis is generally on maintaining social distance, emotional affininty between husband and wife is lacking in many marriages. In fact, there seemed to be an intense dislike between some couples. Nevertheless, the women continued to follow the time-honored custom of eating from the same plate as the husband (after he finishes eating) and following all the deference customs. There seemed to be a separation of feelings and rituals. It is not mandatory that a wife love her husband, but she should follow all rules and perform all the rituals. It was clear that love and affection could not be forcefully extracted from women. On the other hand, deference from the wives was demanded and almost always obtained.

JOKES AND INTERSEX RELATIONSHIPS

The relationship between husband and wife and the general nature of intersex relationships are revealed in the kinds of jokes used by people of the village to amuse themselves. In general, both men and women make fun of women and amuse themselves at their expense. The jokes involve making fun of a woman's body, her mind, and her general nature.

Here are some jokes I heard in Musali. "Women's body and an earthen pot are both the same." "A woman changes her mind three times a second." "A woman says a tiger went by if she saw a mouse go by." "If you give a woman your finger, she will take your whole hand." "When she is good, a woman is very good; but when she is bad she is intolerable." "When a woman opens her mouth even mud turns red hot." "Do not listen to a woman and do not drink alcohol."

Making fun of wives is a favorite hobby of some husbands. It is done quite often, even in front of strangers. Their minds (which are thought of as scatter-brained), their bodies (which are weak and dirty), their dress and their mannerisms and their talk—all are made fun of. Sometimes it can get quite vicious.

Sometimes sisters and other women are also subjected to this. Mothers are generally not made fun of, as it is considered morally offensive. And not all men resort to such behavior, but it is not considered improper to do so, since it is thought of as good, clean fun.

Another common topic for jokes is the henpecked husband. Men are very sensitive about being considered henpecked. All men try to establish their hegemony over women in every possible way and to make sure it is visible to everyone. Ordering wives around in front of others, making derogatory jokes about them, and having fun at their expense are some ways this is done. If women meekly accept it or join in, they have proved their point.

Women's reactions to such attitudes and behavior on the part of men are varied. The most common one is to bear it silently. As several women told me, there is no point in spoiling the fun they are having. If you do not agree, just pretend you did not hear it. It is for the best that women do not say anything about anything. As her tongue is a woman's enemy, the better she controls it, the better off she will be. Another reaction of women is to join in the fun themselves. Many women actively participate in denigrating themselves and laugh with the men, which seems to be very satisfying to the men. The third kind of reaction is protest. Sometimes it is mild, and at others it tends to be pronouced. The woman who resorts to this does it at her own peril. There have been many cases where women have been beaten, sometimes very seriously, for this kind of behavior. This third alternative is generally taken by a very small minority of Vokkaliga women, while it is rare among Brahmins.

Among the Vokkaligas, women work very hard, sometimes harder than their men. Some of these men are lazy, and a few are habitual drinkers. It is often in such cases that women refuse to accept ridicule from the men. It is precisely these men who are afraid of losing their prestige and standing among their peers and wish to establish overtly that they are the rulers of the house despite their meager economic contribution. Severe beatings occur when a women protests too hard, with the result that she is forced to accept that he is the lord and master. She is told that without the physical strength to defy him, she had better accept his overlordship. If the beatings are excessive and if the woman is judged as not deserving such punishment, the fathers and brothers of the women or the village elders might choose to intervene, even though reluctantly, to advise the husband to be moderate. Most often, public opinion favors the husband. Men generally stick together and do not tolerate any intrusion on their unquestioned superiority. Other women either do not say anything or admonish her for her stupidity in bringing such a fate over herself by her inability to handle her husband through manipulation. Dyavamma, one of my Vokkaliga respondents, was completely convinced that it is not a difficult thing to do if you are smart (see Appendix A, Case History 46). She also was of the opinion that women should learn to take care of themselves and not depend on anyone. Since it is an accepted dictum that it is unfeminine for a woman to question male authority, she receives no support from men or women. Yet some protest too often, and the beatings continue; they gradually become less frequent only as the woman begins to give in.

Chapter V

THE DAILY LIFE OF BRAHMIN AND VOKKALIGA WOMEN

The details of daily life, which differ significantly for Brahmin and Vokkaliga women, are presented in this chapter. The discussion is separate for each of the two castes. In addition to normal daily activities, leisure time activities and economically remunerative activities are described. These latter topics are discussed together for both castes since there are many similarities.

BRAHMIN WOMEN

A Brahmin woman gets up from bed before the sun and usually before everyone else in the family. She then washes her face, puts *Kumkum* (red auspicious mark only women with living husbands are allowed to wear) on her forehead, cleans the threshold of the house by dusting it and purifying it with a mixture of cow dung and water, and decorates it with *Rangole* (white powder). The cleaning and decoration of the threshold is believed to bless the whole household.[1]

The stove (usually made of either mud or stone) in the kitchen is cleaned by removing yesterday's ashes, dusting and purifying with water-cow dung mixture, and decorating it with *Rangole*. Then the same thing is done to the kitchen floor. The next job is to prepare coffee in the kitchen and start the fire (usually using firewood or cow dung cakes) in the bathroom to heat water for baths. Even though some water is usually

49

stored in the bathroom, more water needs to be carried in, as everyone in the house has to take a bath every day and change clothes. After giving coffee to everyone and drinking a cup herself, she brings water into the bathroom.

Yesterday's dishes are then washed, using tamarind (a sticky sour fruit) and ash, and rinsed thoroughly with water. Afterwards, she takes a bath with warm water (or if they cannot afford firewood, with cold water), puts on fresh, ritually pure clothes that have been washed and dried in a special place where no one touches them. Then water is brought to the kitchen in ritually pure pitchers. These pitchers are washed with tamarind and no one is allowed to touch them.[2] If the family owns cows that give milk, milking is usually done before one takes the bath. It actually can be done even after the bath as the cow is like god and therefore always ritually pure. But in many households it is done before the bath because one may run into persons who are ritually impure, because the cowshed is located some distance away from the house, or because Śudras are employed to clean the shed.

The next job is preparing the breakfast. This usually consists of *rotti* (a kind of bread made of millet in poor households, rice or wheat in well-to-do households) along with some pickle or *chutni* (spicy sauce). If they can afford it, *ghee* (clarified butter) or *mosaru* (curds) may be served with the *rotti*. Many poorer families these days have been selling their milk to the dairy and have none left for preparing curds or *ghee*. They may have some *majjige* (skimmed buttermilk) instead. Generally, the man who does the plowing gets a special portion of *ghee* and curds, as do the eldest sons who are ready for doing the farm work. The youngest child in the family also gets privileged treatment. The others have to be satisfied with whatever they can get unless there is enough for everyone in the family. In some families the leftover rice from the previous night is used for breakfast with some spices added to it. If there is leftover soup from the day before, it is served along with the rice. Children are usually given breakfast first, along with the men. Women eat at the end.

Before eating breakfast, the family deity is worshipped every day by the head of the household. Since he is worshipping the god on behalf of everyone, children usually join in only at the tail end of the *puja* (worship). This may take anywhere from five minutes to an hour depending on which day of the week it is (Saturday or Monday being the longest) and whether it is a special auspicious day. It is the woman's job to clean the *puja* house, pick flowers for the ceremony, and in general keep everything in readiness for her husband to do the worshipping. The women do the *puja* after serving everyone breakfast and before they have eaten. They have their breakfast after the *puja*, unless it happens to be a day of fasting.

Among the daily chores are washing clothes and sweeping the

house. If there are several women in the house, the labor is generally divided—one doing the kitchen work and the other doing the outside work. If not, the same person sweeps in the morning and washes the clothes in the afternoon. If the woman has daughters, they generally help her out in doing odd jobs around the house.

The midday meal is the main meal of the day. It usually consists of rice and vegetable curry, buttermilk, pickle, and perhaps some *ghee*. Buttermilk used for the meal is generally quite watery, made from the portions left after butter is skimmed out of curds. A meal is not considered a meal unless one ends it with rice and buttermilk. In poorer families *hittu* (cooked millet flour in the shape of balls) is eaten along with rice. The vegetables used are spinach, beans, eggplant, or different kinds of squash which are usually mixed with cooked lentils. When available in the market or in one's own farm various types of pulses are used. Some families have a small kitchen garden where the women grow vegetables such as chilis (hot peppers), and coriander plants. Others buy herbs at the weekly fair in Hosoor. Spices are always added to the vegetables to make them savory. There are several kinds of spices that can be added, and women use their ingenuity and try to have variety over the week.

In almost all families the same curry is used for both the midday and night meal, along with *hittu*, and rice. The midday meal is eaten at about 1:30 P.M. The woman first serves everyone and then eats herself, cleans the floor, and washes the dishes. By now it is about 3 P.M. and time to get things ready for the next day. Rice and pulses are to be cleaned and flour made. Tomorrow's breakfast may be *dosa* or *idli* (different types of rice cakes) which require overnight fermentation and therefore have to be planned today. One also generally needs a *chutni* to serve with the breakfast. Afternoon coffee is prepared around 4 P.M.

In the evening, meal preparation for the night starts. Evening meals themselves do not take very long to prepare, because, as mentioned above, the afternoon curry is used again and only rice or *hittu* needs to be prepared. Cows, if any, are milked, and the milk heated and set to ferment into curds for the next day. Candles are lit in the *puja* house and prayers said. The evening meal is taken usually around 9 P.M. Just as in the afternoon the men and children eat first and the women afterward. The floor is cleaned, the dishes are kept aside to be cleaned tomorrow. The beds are rolled out about 10 and everyone is asleep by about 11.

This is the general routine of daily activities, although there are some variations because of unique circumstances of each household. Women with young children have the additional task of caring for them. The children have to be fed at the proper time, bathed every day, and their clothes changed twice or more every day. Although women generally do not have time to play with the children, all their needs are very carefully looked after. Mothers with small children do not observe ritual purity very scrupulously, because it is very difficult to avoid touching children when cleaning them. Women without small children observe the rituals all through the day. Sometimes, clothing is made for the children with some special kind of fiber which is considered nonpolluting.

Brahmins observe a number of festivals, and a festival always means extra work for women. It usually involves special dishes for offering, special types of garlands with cotton and flowers, and different types of incense. Special meals have to be prepared to recognize the day. Extra cleaning has to be done. Usually at least one sweet dish is prepared. Sometimes guests have to be invited and served. Many women start preparations for particularly important festivals weeks ahead of time. Often these festivals call for fasting for at least half a day, which means the women have to do the extra work on an empty stomach. Besides, they can eat only one meal on the festival day itself.

In addition to the daily routine and special festival occasions, there is extra work for the women in particular seasons of the year coinciding with the harvest of various crops. During *Adake Suggi* (Oct.-Nov.) arecanut has to be cured and processed; during *Hunase Suggi* (Dec.-Jan.), tamarind has to be cleaned and processed and stored away. There are particular months of the year when pulses and grains are harvested, cleaned, processed, and stored away. For pulses, extra care has to be taken in storing to minimize the problem of pests.

If there are several women in the house, the work is shared and things go on relatively smoothly. But where there is only one woman, she is usually overworked as no help is available from anywhere. This is especially true of mothers with small children.

VOKKALIGA WOMEN

The routine of daily activity of Vokkaliga women is similar to that of Brahmin women in many respects but there are several exceptions. First, Vokkaliga women do not worry about ritual purity. They take a bath only once a week, as do all the other members of the family including children. This cuts down on washing clothes, carrying water for the bath, and so on. Also, the whole house is cleaned only once a week, which further cuts down the work. The floor is swept clean and cooking utensils are washed every day, however.

A Vokkaliga woman also gets up before everyone else, cleans the threshold, and decorates it. Most Vokkaligas have not developed the coffee-drinking habit. Still, every morning the kitchen has to be cleaned, cooking stoves cleaned, the cattle fed, and the cows milked.

In the afternoons the cleaning and preparing of vegetables, pulses,

A VOKKALIGA WOMAN DECORATES THE THRESHOLD OF HER HOUSE EVERY DAY, TO
OBTAIN A BLESSING FOR THE WHOLE HOUSEHOLD.

and grains are done. Spices are prepared. Women used to grind the grain
every day to make flour for preparing *rotti* and *hittu*, but since the opening
of the flour mill and rice mill ten years ago, most of the village women
use these services. But there are still three Vokkaliga families where
mothers-in-law insist that their new daughters-in-law grind the grain
every day. The mothers-in-law in these families are known to be very
demanding towards their daughters-in-law.

The Vokkaligas do not celebrate as many festivals as Brahmins. There
is no daily worship in the family. Occasional visits to the temple are all
that is required. On special festival occasions, such as *Pitri Paksha*, *Nagar
Panchami*, *Sankranti*, *Yugadi*, and *Shashti*, visiting the temple is obligatory.[3] The meal preparation is never elaborate. A special kind of meat
has to be prepared on certain festival occasions like the *Mariamma Habba*
(annual festival of the village goddess).

Daily meals include *rotti* in the morning with hot pickles. The afternoon meal often consists of *hittu* (sometimes a little rice as well) with
kalu (pulse) or *bele* (lentil) soup and with any available vegetable, such
as spinach, eggplant, or beans. The *saru* prepared in the afternoon will
do for the evening meal also, except that fresh *hittu* or rice is prepared.
Meat, although it is a luxury, is considered obligatory when guests arrive,
which happens quite frequently in some families. Normally families try

to consume meat once a week. On festival occasions, sweets and meat are also prepared. The type of attention given to men and serving procedures are similar to those of Brahmins, with men doing work outside the house and women inside the house.

When there are several women in the house, the work is often shared, those with small children taking care of household chores and others, particularly the older women, doing the farm work. With a single woman in the house, the entire burden of household work as well as farm work falls on her alone.

Comparison of life-styles in the two castes is important because as the lower castes become more affluent they adopt upper-caste values and behavioral patterns.

Material conditions are important in determining the nature of women's participation in productive work outside the home. The reproductive labor is carried on by women exclusively in all castes. If the men are economically well off, the women are not required to participate in productive labor, which is the case in most families in upper castes. But in the lower castes where the men find it difficult to make ends meet, women's labor in productive activity is required. Once the men become capable of supporting their families they require their women to restrict

VOKKALIGA WOMEN PERFORM THEIR MORNING CHORES WHILE THE MEN WATCH.

their activities to reproductive work only. It is considered prestigious for women to be excluded from productive labor because it is more like upper-caste behavior and also because it reduces the drudgery.

Men's work and women's work are clearly defined among Brahmins, and men doing women's work or vice versa is very rare. Among Vokkaligas, plowing, driving the bullock cart, carrying heavy loads, and managing the farm work are exclusively men's work; housework, childcare, gathering firewood for cooking are exclusively women's work. On the other hand, carrying cow dung and fertilizer to the farm, sowing, planting, cleaning and curing of pulses and grains, harvesting of grain, and taking care of cattle can be done by either men or women. Women are generally expected to help men in the farm work; only women with small children with an excessive amount of housework are excused from farm work.[4]

LEISURE-TIME ACTIVITIES

The major leisure-time activities of the Vokkaliga women are grooming themselves and visiting with other women. They usually wash their hair once a week when they take a bath and use castor oil in their hair two or three times a week.[5] A favorite pastime for a woman is to comb her hair, put castor oil in it, and after the midday meal get together with other women and chew betel nuts and leaves with tobacco, *kaddi-pudi* (herb mixtures), and gossip a bit. Most women do not get time to do this often but cherish these few moments. Older women may also get together in each other's houses once in a while after the evening meal and chew betel leaves together. Chain chewing of betel leaves is indulged in by older women, whereas younger ones tend to do it two or three times a day. The herb mixture contained in the chewing material leaves a thick black coating on the teeth of many women. It is believed that the coating, although somewhat unseemly, helps keep the teeth strong and healthy. Most women are addicted to the chewing habit and say they are unable to give it up. More importantly, they do not want to give it up as it relieves tensions and anxieties in life and makes them feel good.

In addition to chatting about various things, these women may also groom each other by combing each other's hair. The topics of chat generally might be about the mannerisms of a new bride who has come to the village, the marriage arrangements which are going on in different families, new guests in the village, mother-in-law problems, newborn babies and pregnant women, and the sex lives of different people. While talking and chewing, many women do handicrafts like mat making, curing vegetables, and mending clothes. On rare occasions they get together and sing folk songs, the themes of which range from the sorrow felt by parents when the daughters leave the *thavaru* after marriage, brother-sister love, and the agonies suffered by the young bride in the new home to the general predicament of being women. These women get so involved in this singing that most of them cry continuously as the singing is going on. When asked why they did this, the answer was that they felt that they themselves were going through these experiences all over again.

The leisure-time activities of Brahmin women are similar to Vokkaliga women in some respects. For example, chatting is the most common form of leisure-time activity of Brahmin women, and the topics discussed are also similar. Sometimes additional topics figure in the converstaion, such as a son's education, comparison of life in villages and towns, the availability of transportation facilities in the village for children attending schools in towns. Compared to Vokkaliga women, Brahmin women are less relaxed and tend to feel guilty if they spend time getting together in other women's homes. They generally try to find some pretext or other like borrowing a cup of sugar or helping each other in cooking to visit each other. However, getting together for religious reasons is considered proper. This is done once every two or three months when *Harikatha* sessions (songs and stories about gods, goddesses, and Pativratas) are held. Brahmin women do not sing folk songs, only religious songs. The frequency of these meetings used to be once in fifteen days on *Ekadasi* (the eleventh day of the moon) but this is no longer so. The reason seems to be that there are not many women who sing these songs any more. Brahmin women chew betel leaves, nuts, and lime without the other ingredients used by Vokkaliga women, usually once after the midday meal and rarely after both meals.

ECONOMICALLY REMUNERATIVE ACTIVITIES

Some Brahmin and Vokkaliga women undertake financially remunerative activities such as making handicrafts. These include making of leaf cups and plates among Brahmins and making of straw and leaf mats and baskets among Vokkaligas. Middlemen make a large profit through the sale of these handicrafts, and the women themselves get only a fraction of the market price. Brahmin women are particularly vulnerable since they are not allowed to go out of the house and engage in activities like selling things. Younger and inexperienced Vokkaliga women suffer the same fate. But some older Vokkaliga women venture to sell the products themselves.

In addition to handicrafts mentioned above, curing of arecanut is one activity of Brahmin women that is financially rewarding. This work is labor intensive and monotonous. The entrepreneurs who deal with this product exploit the women and pay as little as they possibly can— often less than 25 percent of the standard minimum wage. Since Brahmin

A VOKKALIGA WOMAN WEAVES A LEAF MAT, ONE OF THE FEW INDEPENDENT ECONOMIC ACTIVITIES AVAILABLE TO VILLAGE WOMEN.

women are not allowed to go outside the home for work, they are forced to earn whatever they can within the house. Women are not united in any way to bargain for a better wage.

Some Vokkaliga women had to work for wages just to make ends meet. Invariably they earned 60 percent or less of what men earned for the same or similar jobs. In addition, they are the last ones to be hired and first ones to be fired. In rare cases a woman has an independent source of a small income such as a milking cow or a buffalo given as a gift by her parents or brothers.

In all cases, among both Brahmins and Vokkaligas, where the women had some source of income, the husbands reserved the right to appropriate it. In some cases they in fact did appropriate it as a matter of principle. It usually took the form of men not buying the women their yearly supply of necessary clothing for daily wear or other necessities, thereby forcing the women to spend their own money. Some women responded to these strategies by refusing to do the extra work, but frequently such options were not open.

Chapter VI

SOCIALIZATION OF WOMEN THROUGH THE LIFE CYCLE 1: PREPARATION FOR AND ARRANGEMENT OF MARRIAGE

The ideology of Pativratya affects the socialization of women throughout the life cycle. The general tenor of the practices is similar in both Brahmin and Vokkaliga castes, though there is some variation in details. The focus is continuously to make women understand their position in relation to men and to convince them that their postion is legitimate. Since there is consensus among everyone in charge regarding the proper role of men and women and their interrelationship, no meaningful opportunity for questioning socialization practices exists.

METHOD OF SOCIALIZATION

Both inducements and threats are used to make boys and girls conform to the preferred mode of behavior. Actual physical punishment is rare, but, depending on the age of the child, various devices such as the bogeyman, threats of corporal punishment, and putting the child to shame are employed. One important and revealing aspect of the process is that the types of behavior and the set of values that parents try to inculcate in their children are different for boys and girls. In addition, the methods used to obtain conformity are also different. Little boys and girls soon learn that the same behavior in similar circumstances may bring praise or disapproval, depending upon gender.

The best form of discipline to promote conformity to expected behavioral patterns is believed to be comparing the child to other exemplary children: "See how good (dutiful, obedient, hard working) that child is. Don't you want to be like that too?" Sometimes, when a child is small, inducements are provided in the form of candies or praise. If that does not work, the child is threatened with the approach of *Gummayya* (the bogeyman) who carries off little boys and girls if they misbehave. Minturn and Hitchcock (1966) also observe such patterns of behavior in their study. These methods are used until a child is about five years of age. For an older boy, up to about ten years of age, more severe threats like complaining to the father may be used. Shaming as a tactic is widely used both by parents and by primary school teachers. One teacher, for example, compelled students who failed their exams to crawl between the legs of a smart boy. Even worse, he once had a smart girl slap errant boys on their cheeks, an experience the boys considered most humiliating. These measures are considered unnecessary for girls who are believed to be very easily persuaded. Besides, schoolwork is not as important for girls as learning housework and good manners.

Mothers do not physically punish their children very often, though it does happen on occasion. When it does happen, it is not so much a systematic administration of punishment to teach the child about his or her wrong doings but is often an impulsive reaction triggered by many frustrations unrelated to the child's behavior. It may be that her husband slighted her, her mother-in-law needled her, or for any number of similar reasons that the mother may beat her child. Carstairs (1961) also observes that mothers tend to behave impulsively towards their children. Very often little children are at a loss to understand why their mothers are so angry. Soon, of course, they learn to keep away from her when she is angry. Boys tend to be victims of such impulsiveness more frequently, possibly because the girls seem to learn quickly to read the cues on their mother's face. It may also be possible that girls conform, whereas boys tend to defy their mothers more often.

In order for children to become proper young men and women, parents and other elders should give proper advice, make sure that their children keep proper company, and act as examples of proper behavior and honesty. Different advice is given to boys and girls, however. With regard to bad company, boys pose problems more often than girls, since girls are denied freedom of movement once they reach the age of ten. From then on, girls are under the direct supervision of their mothers or mother surrogates. Boys, on the other hand, have more freedom of movement and are therefore more likely to fall into bad company. The parents have to endeavor to control their choice of companions and friends. With regard to the third requirement, the demands are stringent. Especially in the case of girls, the people of Musali believe "like mother, like daughter." The mother has to watch her own behavior very carefully. When the time comes for arranging marriage, the first person people look at is the mother and her reputation as an indicator of the character of her daughter.

The behavior of adults is monitored by themselves according to the ideals that are cherished by the community. Public opinion favors maintaining conformity. Deviant conduct is severly punished through public disapproval like ridicule, gossiping, and joking, in severe cases through social ostracism.

LIFE-CYCLE CEREMONIES

Brahmin

The life-cycle ceremonies dramatize the different roles played by the two sexes and the different degrees of importance given to them. Among the Brahmins life-cycle ceremonies for boys are many, signifying their movement from one stage of life to the other. These ceremonies are believed to smooth the journey of a man's soul from here to the hereafter. All of these ceremonies involve the chanting of *mantras* (sacred religious hymns) thereby giving the ceremonies religious significance. These ceremonies are: *jatakarma* (birth ceremony); *namakarana* (naming ceremony), celebrated before the baby is six months old; *annaprashana* (first meal), when the child is about one and a half years old; *chaula* (first hair cut) and the *akshara abhyasa* (initiation to learning) when he is about five; *upanayana* (religious initiation) between eight and fifteen years; *vivaha* (marriage), generally after he is eighteen; *prastha* (nuptials), after marriage as soon as the girl becomes physically mature; and *anthyakarma* (funeral). The first five ceremonies are performed when the male is single, the sixth and seventh along with his wife, and the eighth after death. None of the first five ceremonies is considered necessary for a woman as she is classified along with Śudras, which denies her the right to recite Vedic hymns. Even during marriage and nuptials she is only a silent partner insuring the safe spiritual journey of her husband. A woman's funeral ceremonies are performed along with recitation of sacred hymns by the son.

There are several other ceremonies that are conducted which do not have the same religious significance. These ceremonies are intended to insure a safe and good life in this world. The crib ceremony (for both boys and girls), the puberty ceremony (for girls only), the pregnancy ceremony (for women only when they are around seven months pregnant), and widowhood ritual (for women only) are of this type.

Vokkaliga

The Vokkaligas perform only those ceremonies that insure good and safe life in this world but do not have the same spiritual significance as those performed for Brahmin men. These ceremonies include first haircut for boys and girls; puberty ceremony for girls only after their first menstruation; marriage generally after the man is at least eighteen and after the girl's first menstruation; nuptials after marriage; pregnancy ceremony for women only when they are around seven months pregnant; and funeral after death.

STAGES OF THE LIFE CYCLE

In the following pages the socialization of girls at each stage of their life cycle is described. The various life-cycle ceremonies girls or women go through in both castes are described as well. The stages are discussed for both castes in common and the observed differences between castes are pointed out.

Childhood

Birth of a baby At the birth of a baby, one can easily tell if it is a boy or a girl merely by observing the behavior of the people in the family and the general tenor of the surroundings. The whole environment will be suffused with jubilation and a stream of visitors in the case of the birth of a boy. If the baby is a girl, the spirit of the occasion is very subdued. In cases where there are already too many daughters, the faces of people will be downcast, and the whole environment is filled with disappointment and sadness.

Kirtigobba maga arathigobbalu magalu (A son for the pride of the family and a daughter to decorate the house), a slogan used in the family planning campaign, succinctly summarizes the kind of differential importance placed on boys and girls. The son evokes feelings of pride, anticipation, fulfillment, hope, and elation. These feelings generally increase with the number of sons. The daughter, on the other hand, evokes feelings of pity, concern, and affection. Many mothers told me that they cried every time they had a daughter. That cry was as much for themselves—it meant much burden and expense—and also for the little girl who has to go through a life of suffering. One mother remarked, "As soon as I found out it was a girl, I said, 'Oh God, another sinner is born. How can I bear to see her suffer?' " Even though a daughter means a pleasant and positive influence on the quality of life, since she makes life tender and sweet, the realization that she is a transient member of the family puts her in a marginal position. The family has the responsibility to train her properly so that she will bring a good name for the family. But the painful feeling is always there that the parents have to go through a lot of trouble to see her settled and watch her suffer if things do not go right for her.

Crib ceremony   The crib ceremony, when the baby is placed in a crib for the first time, is celebrated about the eleventh day after birth for boy and girl babies in similar fashion among Brahmins. The boys' ceremony is the model, the girls' is the variation. The basic objective of the ceremony is to remove the evil eye and invoke the blessings of all benevolent deities for the protection of the baby in the crib. The crib is worshipped, and songs are sung to invoke the deities.

During my stay in the village, the crib ceremony for baby Sandhya, daughter of Janaki and Venkatesh, was performed. During the ceremony the baby was ceremonially placed inside the crib after god Ganapathi was worshipped.[1] An elaborate song was sung as the baby was placed in the crib and rocked. Only a few people attended the ceremony, and only one sweet was served, along with a banana. Janaki's mother-in-law made it a point to explain to me that I should really have been present during the crib ceremony of her grandson, now two years old. I was told that it was an occasion to remember as there were at least 100 guests and two sweets were distributed, along with coconuts and *ushli* (a delicacy made out of pulses). She further remarked that I should really write in my "book" about her grandson's ceremony rather than that of her granddaughter. I noticed that there is no song portraying the placing of the girl baby into the crib. The song is composed in the name of the boy baby "Gunda." The same song is used for girls also. When I asked why there are no songs for girls, I was told that no special song is necessary for the girl as whatever there is for the boy will do for her.

As far as babies are concerned, not much difference in treatment is apparent. Little children are generally not allowed to cry for too long; they are usually carried around on the hips by mothers or mother surrogates. Weaning and toilet training are done quite gradually, children being easily excused for "accidents." Wiser and Wiser (1971) also observe a similar permissive attitude and behavior in their study. Feeding, weaning, and toilet training are done at similar ages for both boys and girls. Children are breastfed until they are about two and a half or until the next pregnancy, whichever comes first. Toilet training starts around the age of one and a half and the child is generally trained by age three. There seems to be some difference in the attitudes and sentiments shown towards boys and girls: the mother provides for all the baby's needs with relish in the case of boys but does it as a routine in the case of girls.

First haircut   Among the Vokkaligas the first haircut is performed when the child is between one and four years old. This ceremony is supposed to insure good health for the baby by keeping the bad spirits away. An oath is taken when the child is a baby to give the hair to the parents' favorite goddess. At a prearranged time this hair is ceremonially cut and offered to the goddess. The child is taken to different villages according to the oath taken by families. The ceremony is performed for both boy and girl babies in a similar fashion.

The general opinion is that there is a difference between boys and girls in terms of the need for care, attention, and discipline. Boys are believed to be more mischievous than girls; this is considered natural as Lord Krishna (the divine incarnate of Vishnu) himself as a child displayed such behavior. Women feel very proud when they exchange notes about the mischievous behavior of their sons. Whose son is more like *thunta Krishna* (mischievous Krishna) seems to be at stake, as each recites with great embellishment the pranks of her sons. There are a number of songs affectionately and proudly sung by women which depict the deeds of *bala Krishna* (Young Krishna). These range from stealing butter and milk to making a mess of things, getting other people into trouble, breaking things, and giving his mother a lot of hassle through many temper tantrums. While mothers make a virtue out of their sons' misdeeds and stubborness, girls are expected to be very obedient, well behaved, calm, and quiet. Mothers never talk about any misdeeds of their daughters even if they do occur. Such behavior is firmly discouraged among girls, whereas boys get subtle and sometimes even overt encouragement. For example, when a little girl plays in the mud and makes a mess of her dress, she is yelled at, scolded, and firmly told not to do it again. The same behavior on the part of a boy, however, may bring some scoldings, but there is no firmness in the disapproval. Later, he is compared to *thunta Krishna* and bragged about with a neighbor or friend while present. Boys get clear cues from their mothers' behavior that their own mischiefs are not only tolerated by the mother, but actually enjoyed by her. Girls, on the other hand, get considerable praise when they are obedient and quiet. Mothers believe that boys need extra attention, care, and discipline while girls almost grow up by themselves. Boys are also believed to be more susceptible to diseases.

Boys are fussed over and indulged in. This is true in day-to-day life as well as when the child becomes sick. If a son does not eat something that has been prepared, his mother will try making something else; if this is not possible, she will try to coax him into eating whatever has been prepared. If a girl does not eat something she is ignored with the explanation that she will eat if she is hungry. This strategy works efficiently—girls do start to eat whatever is available, whereas boys get what they prefer. On special occasions it is usually the delicacies that are preferred by the boys that are prepared.

I once ate breakfast with a family whose son, Manju, refused to eat a particular dish that was prepared that day, saying it did not have the right taste. His mother began to explain how her son has developed such discriminating taste buds. She tried to coax him into eating it, as she was unable to prepare anything else. I asked the boy's sister, Leela, sitting next to him whether she liked the dish. She just replied that taste did not really matter since she would have to go hungry if she did not eat it. When I asked the mother about Leela as a younger child, she replied that Leela would always eat whatever was given her. When I asked whether Leela had taste buds like her son, she said, "Probably not, and it is just as well because women should always learn to accommodate themselves to whatever there is."

Young children do not wear diapers. Girls and boys are similarly dressed in short shirts or dresses until they are about three or four. Boys are dressed in shorts and shirts and girls in dresses after they are about four. There is no stipulation that particular colors are masculine or feminine. The long dresses girls start to wear after they are toilet trained are not very conducive for rough-and-tumble play, and they are generally encouraged to play at sit-down games. Boys are allowed to run around and do whatever they like.

Until children are about ten years old there is no strict segregation of sexes, though girls are encouraged to play with other girls and are discouraged from fighting with boys, even their own brothers. They are often told that girls are nice and do not fight, they respect their older brothers and love and take care of younger brothers just as a mother does.

BRAHMIN CHILDREN PLAY A MARBLE GAME. GIRLS AND BOYS ARE NOT SEGREGATED AT THIS AGE.

In one family I observed, there was only a one year difference between Veena and her younger brother, Ravi. While Ravi was allowed to be mischievous and selfish, Veena was expected to be calm, collected, and responsible. It was acceptable for Ravi to make a mess anywhere and everywhere; Veena not only was not allowed to make a mess but was expected to clean up after her brother. On one occasion Veena was playing with a set of shells, and Ravi, for some reason, wanted it. When they were arguing about it their mother intervened, took the shells from Veena, and gave them to Ravi while telling Veena strictly not to quarrel about little things like that.

Girls gradually do become quiet and retiring and boys assertive. When I distributed some candies to a group of children between three and ten years of age, even though the girls were eager to get it, I could see them waiting very patiently for their turn while the boys pushed and shoved to grab candy from my hands.

By the time they are about ten, rules become more strict, and girls start to move around with women, assisting them in chores like taking care of little children or doing odd jobs like cleaning, sweeping, and washing.

Adolescence

In the pattern of socialization, even though there is consistency in the types of values instilled and emphasized for the two sexes, a relatively permissive attitude prevails towards sex-role differentiation until the age of five. Between five and ten the boys and girls are directed into different channels using mild forms of discipline and instruction.

By the time the children are about ten, they know many rules of sex-role relationship but have not clearly understood the rationale behind them. Adolescence is the stage in which a rigorous rationale is given for this differentiation, and children are impressed with the legitimacy and the inevitability of it all. The methods used are more direct and to the point. Instruction through example plays an important role, as does practical experience. From the age of ten onward children are strictly segregated according to sex, and the taboo on any physical contact between sexes is emphasized.

Puberty Ceremony   Girls generally have their first menstruation when they are between eleven and fifteen. The practical training for womanhood starts at about eleven. The puberty ceremony dramatizes the issues dealt with at this stage.

The ritual during first menstruation is more elaborate among the Vokkaligas than among Brahmins. The girl is given a bath, dressed in fine clothes, and decorated with flowers. A small hut made out of leaves and branches is the scene for the ceremony. All women of the community are invited to participate, and word is spread about the girl's coming to womanhood. Each guest is expected to bring a present—several copras (dry coconuts), several blocks of jaggery, bananas, sesame seed, and flowers. The present can be a piece of clothing, a utensil, or cash. Families keep track of who gave what and what the cost is, so that they can reciprocate when it is their turn to give presents. This custom, called *muyyi*, is expected by everyone. The value of the presents depends upon both financial status and how closely the families are related.

The women sing songs elaborating themes about the meaning of becoming a woman. The girl is made aware that she is now ready for marriage and her future husband is eagerly awaiting to spend his first night with her. The songs also elaborate how a woman should behave— the qualities of docility, shyness, patience, and tolerance are stressed as being the most important qualities of a woman. She can no longer behave frivolously as she did when she was little. After the songs, to remove the evil eye, a red solution and two oil lamps are taken around the girl's face. The guests are given sweets and flowers. During my stay in the village, Nagarathna from the Vokkaliga community attained puberty. Since she is from a relatively well-to-do family quite a few guests were invited, and the presents she got included stainless steel utensils, *sarees*, blouse pieces, and about 200 rupees, in cash.

From that day on, the girl is secluded inside the house for six months. She is given lots of milk, *ghee*, copra, bananas, and sweets made from sesame and jaggery every day. All of this *araike* (taking care) is supposed to help her body attain its proper feminine shape. She is not allowed to do much hard work and is encouraged to do artistic things like embroidery and bead work. She learns songs and listens to stories about great Pativratas and learns all the good manners required to become a proper wife. The older women in the household take active interest in instilling proper dispositions and attitudes in her. It is made very clear to her that the impulsive carefree days of childhood are over and it is time that she train herself to become a woman. From then on, she is not allowed to go anywhere alone. Permission from adults is mandatory even when she goes chaperoned. She is discouraged from talking to strangers, particularly men, and is no longer allowed to sit in male company. She is told to pay more attention to how she dresses and combs her hair. She is given lessons in cooking and housekeeping. At this stage she is no longer just observing but is learning her future role actively by doing.

After six months of *araike* she begins to do all the household chores. She acts as an apprentice for a while but very soon is expected to take over and have the major responsibility in running the house. This training of a daughter is considered of utmost necessity by every mother. The argument is that the daughter will soon become a wife and will go to live with a mother-in-law. No mother wants to be accused of not teaching her daughter everything there is to know for becoming a proper woman. It is a matter of family prestige. Even in cases where there are several women in the house, the younger daughters are given complete responsibility of running the house so that they have on-the-job training before they are married and sent to a husband's house.

The spirit of the puberty ceremony is the same among Brahmins even though it is not very elaborate. The guests are not expected to bring any presents but fruits and flowers. The girl is secluded, the evil eye is warded off, and sweets and fruits are distributed to all of the visiting women. But the elaborate singing and a separate hut are missing; a few songs in praise of womanhood and delineating its proper qualities are sung. The *araike* or taking care is done, and the girl is secluded. Strict restrictions on her freedom of movement and a taboo against being among men are observed. With regard to housekeeping, she is never given full responsibility but works only as an apprentice except during the time when the mother or any other woman in charge has her monthly period. The reason for withholding full responsibility all the time is that the older women are very concerned about ritual purity and do not trust her to understand these things well as yet. However, she does all the other work like cleaning and assisting in cooking. She is also given extensive instructions regarding proper womanhood through stories and explicit directions. The older women in the family play a very important part in all these aspects of life.

Menstruation   The importance of this stage of adolescence for the rest of a woman's life becomes clear when the meaning and significance attached to menstruation is understood. Among Brahmins, customs like seclusion of a woman during menstruation and her ceremonious purification afterward dramatically point out to her that her body is susceptible to ritual pollution and that she should be careful with regard to her conduct during this time. A woman can have evil effects on growing things at this time and therefore should be careful not to plant any seeds or seedlings or to go near any young plants. Since she is polluting, she should not go near anyone doing a religious ritual nor should she show her face or let her voice be heard. She is secluded and eats alone in a segregated place which is purified after her period is over. She is believed to have evil magical powers, therefore she should keep away from auspicious occasions such as weddings, otherwise there will be disaster. There are many stories about the ancestors being driven to hell because a descendent became contaminated by his contact with a menstruating woman (seeing her, hearing her voice, letting her shadow fall on him, or having physical contact with her). In one story related to me by a Brahmin woman in the village, the wife started to menstruate when she and her husband were having sexual intercourse. Neither of them became quite aware of it until it was over. The next day the husband had to perform the yearly ceremony for his ancestor, which he did in the prescribed manner. But, instead of his ancestors staying in heaven because of his dutiful action, they were driven down to hell. Such was the evil effect of contact with a menstruating woman. The effect was there even when the pollution happened unwittingly. There is no excuse for knowingly causing pollution, and one just has to suffer for one's indiscretions. People are very fearful about getting polluted and causing pollution. Knowing this, women are exremely careful lest some harm come to anyone because of them.

The woman is secluded for three days starting from the onset of menstruation. During this time she is not allowed to take a bath or change clothes since it would contaminate the water—as the evil in her is very strong at this time. On the fourth day, she takes a bath and goes through a purification ritual. One more bath and ritual on the fifth day is necessary to make her completely pollution free. Only after this can she resume sexual intercourse with her husband.

A ritual called *rishi panchami* is observed by women after menopause (usually when they are in their late fifties) to remove all the ill-effects of the pollution unintentionally caused by them during menstruation. The ritual is an elaborate one involving fasting, long hours of worship, substantial amounts of money given in charity in the form of clothing and utensils, and the feeding of a number of Brahmins.

Among Vokkaligas, the requirements are not as stringent, nor is the occasion so serious. But the belief in the evil effects of the menstruating woman is also prevalent among them. She is not allowed to go into the kitchen nor touch any cooked food. She is allowed to go about her other daily activities after she takes a purifying bath. Even so she is not allowed to plant seeds or go near small seedlings. She cannot have sexual intercourse until the fifth day. She sleeps on a mat, uses a separate plate and cup, and wears old clothing which is washed after her period is over.

A girl comes out of this stage thoroughly convinced of her physical and spiritual inferiority since she is in possession of a pollutable body. She realizes that she is in need of constant protection to maintain her virginity before marriage and purity after marriage. The taboo against physical contact with the opposite sex, prohibition of freedom of movement, and strict segregation of sexes dramatically impress upon her the vulnerability of her body and the need for strict obedience to the rules laid down by elders.

MARRIAGE

The search for a bridegroom generally starts when a girl is between fourteen and sixteen, and she is usually married by the time she is about twenty. It used to be the custom among Brahmins to marry the daughter before she started to menstruate. Some marriages would take place as early as when a girl was five years old. It was considered a matter of pride for the family to marry the daughters before their first menstruation as it is holy and most conducive for insuring the safe journey of ancestors to heaven. *Kanya dana* (giving the gift of a daughter who has not reached physical maturity) is the noblest gift of all, bringing about maximum spiritual merit. In addition it removes the burden on the parents of assuring the virginity of a daughter before marriage (Altekar 1956:60).

A girl finds out that she is a liability to her parents very soon in her life but the time of marriage negotiation forcefully drives that point home. Since a marriage costs anywhere from 5,000 to 20,000 rupees, the burden on the parents is often very heavy.[2] Many of them have to sell off part of their land or go into debt to provide the money. Many parents become overtly hostile towards their daughters at this time because the pressures are so great. In addition to watching her parents suffer from monetary problems and experiencing humiliation as they go from one prospective groom to another to arrange the marriage, she suffers on a personal level. She is discussed by everyone concerned. Her physical features, the way she walks, her abilities and conduct—in short, anything and everything about her—is talked about. This becomes most dramatic when the groom and his people come to interview her. She is often made to walk around serving everyone, asked to sing songs, questioned by everyone just to find out what her speech and mannerisms are like. The groom's people make it a point to find out all about her by speaking with her relatives, friends, and acquaintances. She may have to go through several such interviews before a match is settled upon.

Arranging a marriage is a very complex event. While I was in Musali, I observed three marriage arrangements, one in the Vokkaliga community and two in the Brahmin community. I shall now give brief descriptions of these three cases.

Vokkaliga Arrangements

Sarasu   Sarasu was sixteen when her parents, Chennu (mother) and Ranga (father), decided that it was time they started looking for a groom. The crops had been good for two years in a row, and they had been able to save some money for the marriage. Even though Sarasu was not beautiful, she was reasonably good looking. Besides, Sarasu's family had a very good reputation in the community. Her mother especially was admired for her extraordinary patience in her relationship with her mother-in-law who was known to be very demanding and critical. Chennu was very solicitous and docile with her husband, friendly with neighbors, very diligent, did not gossip, kept the house clean and neat all the time, and took care of the household chores well. The neighbors never heard a quarrel between husband and wife. Sarasu was known to the villagers as a replica of her mother who had taken care to teach Sarasu everything she knew. In addition, Sarasu was a strong and healthy woman. Since the completion of her *Araike* after her first menstruation when she was thirteen years old, Sarasu worked around the house with her mother. For the past six months, housework was her complete responsibility, and Chennu had more time to go and work in the fields along with Ranga. Sarasu had two younger brothers, one twelve and another six; one sister and one brother had died when they were barely three years old. Sarasu was very good at taking care of her two brothers as well as doing all the household chores. Sarasu's parents had no doubt that she would make an ideal wife to some man and bring good name to their family. With enough cash on hand, the search was started.

Chennu had an aunt in the nearby village, Marenhalli, as well as one in her own *thavaru*, Ankapura. Ranga had a maternal aunt in Bastihalli and a paternal aunt in Thimmanahalli. He made sure that he met them all during the weekly fair in Hosoor on Fridays and spoke with them about his intentions of celebrating the marriage of Sarasu. He made it clear to them that he is not a very rich man. He has only two and one-half acres of dry land and one acre of wetland and, of course, he has his two sons to think of and cannot spend too much on Sarasu's marriage. Taking a loan was out of the question because, with two good years of monsoons in a row, the next year was very likely to be bad.

Ranga was ready to celebrate the marriage at a level commensurate with his dignity. He could give his daughter a gold necklace, gold ear studs (which Sarasu was wearing), two *sarees*, and some household utensils. To the groom, he could give either 1,000 rupees in cash to cover all the expenses, or he could buy anything they wanted for that amount. Even if he did just that, with the two big meals and other marriage expenses, the total expense would come close to Rs 8,000.[3] He had the needed grain and pulses and could buy the coconut and banana at a cheaper price from his own village. He had poultry and milking buffalo, as well as several goats that could be slaughtered for the marriage feast. He made it clear to his relatives that he could not spend any more than Rs 8,000. He also made it a point to indicate that his daughter is a very desirable match and any man should consider himself lucky to have her as his wife. He asked for their considered opinion about the kind of bridegroom he could afford with the assets he had (daughter who is a desirable match, Rs 6,000 cash and Rs 2,000 in kind). He asked them (as his wife Chennu had suggested) to explore the possibility of getting at least a pair of gold bangles from the groom's side for Sarasu to match her gold studs and gold necklace.

Sarasu's family belongs to the Mullokkalu, a Vokkaliga subcaste. Even though some Mullokkalu had married out of the subcaste, Ranga did not see any reason for crossing the boundaries when there were enough eligible young men in their own subcaste. It was decided that young men from the Mollokkalu caste only should be considered.

Once the financial boundaries were set, they sat down and dicussed the most desirable match for Sarasu. Several young men were discussed but rejected for various reasons. Some were not good enough for Sarasu, some others had very mean mothers, still others did not have enough land; some had too many brothers and sisters—no mother wants to send her daughter to such a home to work for a large horde, unless it is unavoidable. After two weeks of exploration it was found that there were no suitable matches in either Thimmanahalli or Marenahalli. In Ankpura, the few eligible men belonged to the Dasokkalu subcaste. Only in Bastihalli where Ranga's aunt lived were there about five young men who satisfied most of the requirements.

For further screening the question of personality characteristics were considered. It was thought that the two sons of Ranga's aunt were more competent to answer these questions as they were of marriageable age and knew the five young men in question. After some discussion two of the five were eliminated—one had a quick temper with a tendency to get into fights, and the other was lazy and incapable of hard work. It was decided that the three others should be approached by Ranga's uncle who would report back during the next weekly fair. All of this intial screening took about two months, and the real negotiations only started afterward.

After inquiries, Ranga's uncle reported that the parents of one of the young men were not planning their son's marriage this year as they had a grown daughter; until she was married, the question of their son's marriage did not come up. The other two were willing and expressed interest in looking at Sarasu. It was considered proper to examine the horoscopes before the would-be bride and groom met. Both the horoscopes matched pretty well with that of Sarasu.[4] The big problem of deciding between the two remained. It was agreed that Sarasu could visit her aunt and spend a few days with her and in the meanwhile a situation might present itself when a comparative evaluation could be made. While the plans were crystallizing along these lines it was found that one of the families was not willing to give any gold but the other, Ramu's family, was. The matter was settled, and the meeting of the potential bride and groom was arranged.

Meanwhile, the prospective groom's family had their own relatives check on Sarasu's family. They were very happy to find that Sarasu's mother had a very good reputation in the village, and Sarasu was just like her mother. They were ready to meet with Sarasu and her family.

The meeting was arranged in Ranga's aunt's house. Sarasu cooked many delicacies and served everyone gracefully. All were full of praise for her cooking but more than that, Kalamma (Ramu's mother) was very pleased to see that Sarusu always had lowered eyes, touched all of the elder's feet respectfully, spoke only when spoken to in a soft voice, sat down with her head bent, and served everyone with interest—all of which indicated that she would make a perfect daughter-in-law: docile, solicitous, and caring. Ramu was satisfied with Sarasu's looks and mannerisms.

Ramu's family also had a good reputation in the village. He had a younger brother and two sisters; one of the sisters was already married and living in her in-laws' house and the other was only ten years old. Kalamma was known as a good person. The family had three acres of dry land and no wetland, one milking buffalo, some chickens, and two goats. Ramu was a strong sturdy man although not very good looking. But, as everyone knew, looks are not important for a man. He was known to be very hardworking and good natured and also quite competent in buying and selling things.

Once everyone felt satisfied with the match and all the financial give-and-take was settled, the details of marriage were discussed, and a mutual agreement was reached. At this time, a formal engagment ceremony was performed, making the agreement binding on both parties. The engagement party took place in Ranga's house, as is customary, and most of the villagers belonging to their subcaste were invited. A mutually satisfactory date was set for the marriage which happened to be in the month of June when the pressures of farm work are not very great.

Sarasu's parents were convinced that Ramu was a good match. They knew that with the kind of money they had in hand they could not afford an educated man who would demand a dowry of at least Rs 5,000. Besides, Sarasu could barely write her own name, and she might not feel comfortable in a city environment. She would certainly be happy in the village, especially with her own aunt living in the same village. Her aunt could keep an eye on Sarasu and make sure that she is not abused by her in-laws. Her mere presence in that village, Sarasu's parents knew, would discourage such behavior. Besides, Bastihalli is only four miles away from Musali, and frequent visits would be possible.

For the marriage negotiation to reach this stage, it had taken six months and about twenty trips to different villages by Ranga. Of course, various relatives had provided their input into the proceedings as well. Compared to others this marriage arrangement was considered relatively smooth and uneventful. There are many cases where the negotiations break down even in the final stages.

Sarasu herself did not have much to say about the marriage. She just nodded her assent. She did confide in her close girl friend that she was very grateful for all the trouble her parents took to arrange her marriage. She realized that her husband's family is not very well-to-do and probably was worse off than her family. But Ramu is a hardworking young man. He is sort of good looking, too. Most of all she was happy that her father's aunt was living in the same village. Sarasu had always dreaded leaving her *thavaru* and going to a strange new house. She cried whenever she thought of it. Now that she knew that her favorite grand-aunt would be in the village, she would no longer have to be so afraid. Sarasu also got a number of tips from her to make her life in the new family relatively easy. She found out that her mother-in-law was rather partial to her second son. Even though she liked Ramu, it was Govinda who was dearer to her heart. Ramu's father died when Govinda was still a little boy and that may have brought them closer. She was told that the best way to please her mother-in-law is to be nice to Govinda, who was spoiled. She was also told to watch for her sister-in-law and not say much in front of her as she carries stories. About Ramu himself, everyone thought he was a good man but had a tendency to be reserved and serious. This is perhaps because all the family responsibilities have been on his shoulders since his father's death. Sarasu was told that a good wife like her could make a man relax and that she did not have anything to worry about.

Brahmin Arrangements

Leela   The arrangement of Leela's marriage was a complicated affair. Her family belonged to a Smartha subcaste and her father, Krishnappa, being rather conservative, decided that the groom should be chosen from that subcaste only. Even though the family resides in the village, their aspirations rose above the average level in the village (see Appendix A, Case History 18). Two sons in the family were engineers with good jobs in cities. One daughter had married an engineer. All the other children were also going to school and bent on getting degrees. Leela herself had studied up to the final year of a B.A. The family was in a predicament—their expectations were high but their financial means were meager. Besides, Krishnappa was not very competent in arranging marriages.

Krishnappa expected that his sons would help to pay for the marriage because they had good jobs. His sons, however, felt that it was their father's responsibility to marry off his own daughters. This friction between father and sons had postponed Leela's marriage until she was nearing twenty-five, considered to be too late in the village.

Krishnappa was already overburdened with loans that he had taken for his elder daughter's marriage and was not eager to borrow any more. He was feeling very frustrated that neither his elder brother nor his own sons were coming to his aid in his time of need. Whenever his wife Shanta broached the subject of their daughter's marriage he simply said that whatever fate had ordained will happen. He himself was helpless and could not do anything about the marriage.

Leela, watching all this, had become quite despondent and constantly comtemplated suicide. She told her mother more than once that she would commit suicide if not married before her twenty-fifth birthday. Shanta implored her sons and her sister-in-law in the city to do anything they could to save Leela's life. Finally Krishnappa's brother and his wife agreed to begin looking for a bridegroom and the sons agreed to supply the money necessary for the marriage.

It was agreed that the second son Ramu's marriage should be performed along with Leela's to cut down the cost of the weddings. With regard to the groom's qualifications, it was realistic not to aspire too high, so grooms with an engineering or medical degree (B.E. or M.B.B.S) were considered out of their reach. Such a conclusion was reached after finding out that young men with such high qualifications want brides who have at least a bachelor's degree and demand a dowry which can range from five to fifteen thousand rupees. In addition, Leela, even though good looking, was not considered beautiful as she did not have very fair skin.

Leela was deeply disappointed when she heard about such decisions. The very thought of marrying anyone without high qualifications disgusted her. The thought made her particularly depressed when she compared herself to her elder sister who had married an engineer with a good job. Leela always considered herself better looking and more intelligent than her elder sister. Leela's parents and brothers persuaded her to agree to the decisions since there was no other alternative except to remain unmarried, which was almost unthinkable.

After much exploration a type of exchange marriage was settled in the same subcaste. The groom Raju was five years older than Leela and had a bachelor's degree in commerce (B. Com.). He was from a small town and his family was well-to-do. Raju's aunt's daughter Somi was to marry Ramu, Leela's brother. Everyone was of the opinion that the matches were good. The horoscopes of the two couples had matched. All families had a good reputation. The people were well known in the community as being good, honest, and trustworthy. The two girls were equal in their good looks. The boys had educational qualifications the girls deserved—Ramu had an engineering degree (B.E.) and Somi a bachelor of arts (B.A.). Leela did not have a degree, and Raju had his bachelor's degree in commerce (B. Com.). Leela felt that she was settling for second best but as she had no other options agreed. The marriage expenses were cut down greatly; neither party paid any dowry and the number of presents was kept to a minimum. Each party was expected to take care of all the purchases needed by brides and grooms on their own side. Leela's family spent about 13,000 rupees and the other party about

16,000 rupees. The disparity, it was felt, was justified as the bride on their side was getting a better bargain by marrying an engineer with a job. Leela's two brothers borrowed money for the marriage. The marriage went on smoothly but the loan would probably take several years to be repaid.

This arrangement is not completely typical, though similar problems are encountered by many Brahmins in the village. The fathers generally try to provide for the marriage and might ask for some help from their sons instead of depending on them completely. In such cases aspirations to marry well will be absent since the father cannot afford the expense. In this example, a precedent was set by marrying the elder daughter to an engineer, and the aspiration level of the second daughter had gone up. In addition, searching for a groom is generally done by the father. He might ask for some help from relatives and friends but does not completely rely on someone else. In Krishnappa's family, however, the two brothers had a father-and-son type of relationship due to a wide age disparity between them and their relationship was built on reciprocal obligations.

Exchange marriages are becoming very common among Brahmins as the cost of dowry has become prohibitive. Unless one settles for an uneducated man living in a village without much financial resources or physical attraction, a certain amount of dowry must always be paid. The character and beauty of the girl or her educational and job qualifications might reduce the size of the dowry.

Village girls in general are considered less sophisticated and not good enough for city boys. Though many parents in the village try to make sure that their daughters get at least twelfth grade education and are ready to give dowry, finding an educated groom is difficult. One has to have contacts in an urban area, as Leela did, to push the match through. There was another case that I observed in Musali which illuminates these points.

Padma Padma was a pretty girl, well accomplished in music, who had failed the twelfth grade examination three times. She was the only daughter of her rather well-to-do parents. Their desire was to marry Padma to a well-educated man with a good job, preferably one with M.B.B.S. or B.E. degree. They were ready to pay as much dowry as Rs 10,000. The search was on, and Padma's father was consulting with various people and traveling to different places to find a suitable match.

Padma went through several interviews which she felt were humiliating. She had to sing on each occasion. She had to cook many delicacies to prove that she was a good cook. People continuously stared at her, scrutinizing her every move. Besides, they asked her many questions which sounded very unusual to her. For example, in one interview she was asked who buys her *sarees*. She replied that it was her mother, which was apparently the wrong answer, and she failed that interview. It turned out that the question was intended to find out who the boss in the family was and whether her mother was domineering. The right answer was that both parents took her to the shop and while her mother helped her choose the *saree*, the father paid for it. In another interview, Padma was asked to pick up a small baby who was crying, just to see how she handled the baby and whether she was capable of soothing it. Poor Padma failed again; the baby did not stop crying. She was also rather clumsy in handling the baby since she had no such experience, being the youngest in the family. In another interview she was made to pay respects by touching the feet of some ten men and women assembled in the room who were not directly related to either party. On her own, Padma had touched the feet of her would-be mother-in-law and father-in-law and was about to sit down. But the prospective mother-in-law admonished her to touch the feet of every older person in the room. Padma did that, but the complaint was that it seemed as though she did not like doing it (which was true!). Padma was sick and tired of all these interviews and did not like being examined by so many people. She felt very discouraged because every interview ended in failure.

I tried to find out the reason for these failures. After much probing, I found that Padma's inability to complete even the twelfth grade and her living in the village were definite drawbacks. In addition, her mother's reputation of being a rather domineering woman played a significant part. Padma's performance in the interviews did not help her much either. Finally, the family did not have a competent person to negotiate the marriage.[5]

One can identify the following sequence of events in the process of marriage arrangement. First of all, the pool of eligibles is determined on the basis of membership in the same subcaste and economic status. In addition, educational qualifications are also taken into account among Brahmins[6] and the physical strength and health of both bride and groom among Vokkaligas.[7] The *jatakas* (horoscopes) are then examined for compatibility between the couple for longevity of life for the man and chances of male offspring. After all of these matters are taken care of, a meeting between the two families is arranged where the boy and girl get a chance to see each other. If there is consent of both parties for the alliance, financial transactions are discussed and a date for the marriage set.

Economic assets are one of the most important factors in facilitating the arrangement of marriage. Other important factors are the qualifications of boy and girl and the negotiating skill of those arranging the marriage. Physical beauty is considered less important for the boy and his earning capacity much more important. For a girl, her character and physical beauty are equally important. The character and reputation of the mother of the girl are closely scrutinized as there is a firm belief that daughters turn out like their mothers. Physical beauty—fair skin, long dark hair, long eyelashes, a well-proportioned nose, and wide black eyes—is considered desirable. A well-proportioned body with large breasts, a small waist, and big hips with a small build is considered important. If the girl has a good education or a good job like that of a bank clerk, teacher, or secretary, the size of the dowry is reduced. The amount of dowry to be paid to the groom goes up in proportion to his education.

It is also very important that a family should have negotiating skill to make a good marriage alliance. In Sarasu's case, her grandaunt made sure that Sarasu got a pair of gold bangles from the groom's side. She played a very important role in screening the young men and finally reducing the field of eligibles. She also made sure that both families felt they were making a good alliance by various devices such as praising their good qualities at appropriate times in the right amounts. By her tact she made Ramu's family feel that it was being treated very well by Sarasu's family. Negotiating the alliance needs expertise, finesse, and talent. A good negotiator is in the right place at the right time and says the right things to the right people. The older people in the community and at times some young people with such talents play an important role in this field. In Leela's marriage, it was her aunt (father's elder brother's wife) who did most of the negotiating since she was considered by almost everyone as having such expertise. By the time the negotiations were over she had managed to reduce the marriage expense by Rs 6,000 (about $800).

In spite of the fact that the boy and girl have to meet each other (along with their families, of course) and give their consent for the marriage, it is generally a one-sided affair. The fact that the expenditure is mainly borne by the girl's parents makes her a burden on them. This, coupled with the stigma attached to an unmarried girl of a marriageable age, puts considerable pressure on the girl not to be too particular about her choice. She generally does not object to a boy chosen by her parents, and her assent is only a formality. In fact, at times she is not even asked for an opinion or if she does have an objection she may be overruled by her parents. The lack of real options for the girl under these circumstances tends to make her fatalistic. She makes many compromises in her choice and becomes accommodating.

I talked to a number of women about their experiences and feelings while their marriages were being arranged. Each one of them said it was a period of great anxiety and unhappiness. The account given by Dyavamma is very vivid and expresses the feelings of most others.

> I felt I was a great burden to my parents, especially my father. He resented having so many [four] daughters [on whom he had to spend so much] and only one son. He often complained that

all his toil was only to make others rich and not for his own family. For him, the family did not include his daughters; he used to say that daughters are only born to bankrupt the house. In their helplessness and sorrow, my parents—especially my father—became overtly hostile towards me. I wished myself dead. I wished I was never born. I felt ashamed to look at myself in the mirror and terribly guilty about facing my parents [see Appendix A, Case History 46].

All the mothers I spoke to were sure that daughters were more difficult to bring up mainly due to problems involved in arranging a marriage and the expenses of the wedding. They were sure that while growing up, sons needed more care and attention, since they were more mischievous, got sick more often, and tended to be more demanding. The daughters were still considered a burden, because they were transients and yet necessitated so much expense. It is not that they blamed their daughters but that it is just "in the nature of things"; therefore, it is better to have sons rather than daughters.

Despite all these problems, the institution of arranged marriage is as strong as ever. Even in urban areas, the arranged marriage is the rule rather than the exception. Goldstein (1972:70–85) writes that even university-educated women in urban areas cannot do away with the system of arranged marriages. The adults in the family value the traditional notions of marriage and family.

Chapter VII

SOCIALIZATION OF WOMEN THROUGH THE LIFE CYCLE 2: MARRIED LIFE, OLD AGE, AND WIDOWHOOD

Traditionally marriage meant achievement of adulthood even though the brides used to be very young, especially among Brahmins. Nevertheless, the actual assumption of adult responsbilities took place only after a girl attained physical maturity. At the present time, because there are laws against child marriages, most of the brides are in their teens. In general, they assume adult responsibilities soon after marriage.

MARRIAGE CEREMONY

Many customs and rituals practiced during the marriage ceremony depict the proper relationship between husband and wife. To begin with, a wife is always younger and shorter than her husband. Among Brahmins, a certain ceremony is performed to insure that she will not grow taller than her husband. This involves keeping the *noga* (yoke) on her head while chanting hymns. This ceremony was considered necessary in earlier years especially when the girls were married young. A bride should sit with her head bent wearing a demure look. She always walks behind her husband, again with her head bent, and lets him lead her. By common usage, marriage is expressed as giving the bride away to the groom. This is done ceremoniously by placing the bride's hand in the groom's and pouring water onto her hand.

The couple are made to engage in playful little games which further illustrate her relative position. For example, among the Vokkaligas, the couple is asked to reach into a pitcher filled with water and bring out the things that are inside—a feather, a flower, and a few metal objects. The person who extracts a feather will be a follower, but if one gets out a metal object he/she will be a leader. Naturally the bride should make sure to pull out either a flower or a feather and the groom one of the metal objects. Even though everyone knows the eventual outcome, people enjoy the game thoroughly and comment on how the two will make an ideal couple.

Among Brahmins, the couple is asked to eat from the same plate filled with fruits and drink out of the same cup filled with milk. All the relatives gather around and start to coax the couple. But everyone knows the groom has to make the first move and the bride has to follow him. Finally it does happen and the groom eats a part of the fruit, gives her the remainder, and then drinks part of the milk and gives her the rest. This little game is supposed to signify that the wife has become part of the husband. From then on, the wife was required to eat the leftovers from her husband's plate, after he had finished eating. This rule is still followed by some Brahmin women in Musali.

Various songs are sung by the bride's and groom's people praising the bride and groom respectively and their families. It goes on like a

A VOKKALIGA MARRIAGE CEREMONY.

contest, but the songs are composed in such a way that in the end the bride's people accept their inferiority and concede defeat. In addition, there are many stipulations that the bride's family show deference to the groom's family. For example, the bride's people eat only after all of the groom's people have eaten.

SENSE OF BELONGING

The account given by women when I asked them whether they thought they belonged in the *thavaru* or in their huband's house reveals how they perceive their status in these families. Sundru expressed her opinion in the following words, and her opinion is shared by most women:

> Women do not have a home of their own. They always live in someone else's house, work for someone else. They should always be nice and solicitous if they want to be treated properly. Besides, they have to be lucky to have a good life.

Most women feel the burden of responsibility in their husband's house to be heavy and tend to recall their childhood with nostalgia. Several women broke down and cried when they talked about the fine time they had had in their *thavaru*. One important aspect of their life in *thavaru* was that they were relaxed, free from all criticism. They were not afraid, because everyone loved them. They did not have any responsibilites and led a carefree life. Mother always did all the work. Even when she asked for help, she was as gentle as can be. "After all," she used to say, "your work is cut out for you in your in-laws' place, take it easy over here at least." Visiting the *thavaru* is a treat to the women even after many years of marriage. There is no husband to disturb her sleep, no mother-in-law to nag her, and no sisters-in-law to tell on her.

A woman's position at her in-laws is not so bad if her parents are well-to-do and are concerned about her. Her periodic visits to the *thavaru*, where she is pampered and given presents, indicate to the people in her new home that she has people who are concerned about her and she therefore cannot be abused. Even if the parents of the women cannot directly interfere with affairs in her new home they can help her out indirectly by showing how concerned they are about her and giving her moral support to stand up for her rights. In addition, her husband's visits to her *thavaru* along with her on special occasions, where he is honored as a special guest and given presents, enhance her prestige.

Whenever a reference was made to their *thavaru* by these women, it was done in the most tender terms possible. But, I was told, one cannot live in her *thavaru* for long, simply because one does not belong there.

A woman should be married at the proper time, and after marriage she has to leave the *thavaru* for her husband's house. Many folk songs sung by women depict vividly the sad sentiments experienced by everyone on this occasion. The dominant theme of the songs is the loss suffered by the *thavaru* due to her departure. It loses her pleasant cheerful company, the special glow and the tender touch her presence used to give the whole environment. The parents and brothers recall all the little things she used to do—bringing flowers in, lighting the incense sticks, singing happy songs, and most of all her pleasant conversation. A daughter is like a flower, a cool fragrance, a perfume, tender, sweet, and loving. The songs are vivid and picturesque. The substratum of pathos built into the life of a woman becomes clearly visible in their accounts. She has to be married, she has to live among strangers who may not care for her, she has to leave all those who love her, this must be because it is her destiny as a woman: these are the hard facts of life. Everyone knows that *Magalu male, sose bisulu* (A daughter is like rainfall and a daughter-in-law is like sunshine). Of course she is welcome to visit—more often when the mother is living, but rarely after her death since there is no point in visiting when the mother is not there. *Thayi illada thavaru neerillada kere* (*Thavaru* without mother is like a reservoir without water). So, the *thavaru* is the place which one always cherishes but lives in only until marriage and visits as long as the mother is alive.

It is with her husband that a wife belongs. Nobody can tell her to leave if she is a good wife and bears sons. True, if she cannot bear sons she is not of much use to anyone and will surely be discarded. She cannot blame anyone either, except perhaps her own bad luck. Being a good wife is something she should try very hard to achieve. But there is no guarantee that she will be accepted as such. The theme of a woman's suffering in her new home is vividly elaborated in folklore. Usually, the villains are the mother-in-law and sisters-in-law. The father-in-law and brothers-in-law do not appear in the picture at all, or they are silent accomplices. The husband is often the one to administer punishments when his mother and sisters complain about his wife. The complaints are usually about the wife not being faithful to him, not being mindful of family prestige, not being respectful towards her mother-in-law, talking to neighbors about family secrets, or just being lazy. Sometimes, the husband is portrayed as an unwilling accomplice and at others he takes the initiative to teach her to know her place. The songs have vivid descriptions of the tortures administered to the women like scalding, beating, kicking, and starving. She is often forbidden to visit her *thavaru* and prevented from having any visitors. In more severe cases she might be murdered or driven to suicide.

The songs generally depict extreme cases which occur only occasionally. I came across two situations where wives were murdered by cruel husbands and two women who were driven to suicide. There were many more cases where women suffered from loneliness, fatigue, hunger, neglect, and abuse. Many women explained to me that the first few years of married life, until they bore a son, were a living hell. The main concern was to make their existence in the new home bearable. They were trying to find ways and means of escaping beatings from husbands, getting enough to eat, reducing the number of chores so that they were not completely exhausted by night, and getting enough sleep to enable them to carry on the next day. This was never possible, as they were closely watched by everyone and any shortcoming was promptly punished. They never got enough to eat and were unable to get enough sleep either, because the newly married husband had to get his sexual enjoyment. After all, being a good sexual partner to her husband is one of her sacred duties.

There was general consensus among the women that even after one has tried her very best to be a good wife in every way, including being a good sexual partner and bearing sons, there is no guarantee that she will feel at home in her husband's house. All she can do is try her best and pray a lot and count on her good luck.

All women are very aware that, even though a woman's place is with her husband, the place is her husband's. She has come to her husband's home, and she is living among his people. In the beginning she is not accepted as a member of the family; as years go by, as she has sons, her position becomes more and more secure. Nevertheless the feeling that she is living in someone else's house seems to linger on when one hears the comments of various women. As one woman explained to me, when everything is going all right and everyone is happy and contented, problems do not arise. But when there is misunderstanding and discord, the feeling that she is an outsider comes to the surface. For example, if the wife expresses concern when the husband is not very economical in times of monetary trouble in the family, comments such as the following are made by husbands:

> Who do you think you are? Did you bring everything from your *thavaru*? Don't forget you are eating my food and you don't have anything to call your own.

In other words, she has to know her place. She can suggest or offer advice if asked, but she can never expect anything as a matter of right, especially if the problems involve money. She should be very careful and remember that she does not own anything. She works because it is her duty.

WOMEN AND SEX

It became perfectly obvious after staying in the village for about four months that I could not ask men questions pertaining to sex. It is considered unbecoming for a woman to ask men such questions. I decided to collect this information only from women of both castes. I contacted several women, sometimes in groups and sometimes singly. The younger women of both castes were very hesitant to talk about it. All I could get was a giggle or a nod for an answer. All the information I collected comes from older women who answered my questions in detail, quite freely, and very often added insights into the issues.

I found the attitudes and behavior of people in both castes remarkably similar. The Brahmin women were capable of explaining their ideas in a more sophisticated manner whereas Vokkiliga women put the same ideas in simpler language. To understand clearly the topic of women and sex it is necessary to distinguish between what these women thought was expected of them and what in fact their behavior was like. It is necessary to understand the relationship between attitudes and behavior.

The most important tenet, repeated over and over, is that sex is a man's pleasure and a woman's duty.[1] All these women sincerely believe that men have a stronger sex urge which should be satisified by women. They went to the extent of saying that if the woman does not accommodate, she will be making the man suffer unnecessarily. This is unfair to the man and unbecoming of the woman. It is completely irrelevant whether a woman enjoys it or not. She should always bear in mind that the man took all the trouble to bring a stranger to his house precisely for this purpose.

It is believed as strongly that a woman should not indulge in sex play. It is considered unwomanly to become interested in sex too much. Her role is to accommodate the man and bear his children. A good woman, I was told, never enjoys sex. It is motherhood that is to be enjoyed and cherished by women.

One Brahmin woman explained that there are three types of women, namely *shankini*, *padmini*, and *dakini*, according to the *Shastras* (sacred scriptures). The first type is a frigid woman who is incapable of making a man happy. She is for all practical purposes a useless woman. The third type is an indulgent one. She makes a man unsure of himself, enjoying sex too much herself. She might even make demands on the man, which will only make matters worse. A man cannot trust a woman who enjoys sex too much. This would make him worry about being unable to satisfy the woman enough and suspect that she might become unfaithful. Such a relationship will not be conducive to a good marriage. Besides, children born of these two types of women will have undesirable characteristics. The son born of the *shankini* will be incapable of expressing himself, while the son born of the *dakini* type will be too sensual and indulgent, lacking in a sense of duty. It is the second type of woman who is ideal.

Padmini is always a willing participant in sex play but never takes the intiative. She does anything and everything her husband wants her to do during the sex act. The man takes the lead and directs the woman to accommodate him in particular ways, which she cheerfully does. Satisfying her husband is her ultimate goal, and she does it very willingly and tactfully. Sons of superior quality will be born to the *padmini* type.

Vokkaliga women described the same ideas in other words. According to one of them, a man cannot have fun with a frigid woman and he will soon discard her and marry another woman. An indulgent woman will only be asking for trouble. She will make the man suspicious, and he will never let her out of his sight. Besides, he cannot respect a woman who behaves like an animal. On the other hand, if the woman behaves modestly and accommodates her husband in every way he wants her to, he will feel satisfied and will accept her as part of his family gradually even though she comes to him as a perfect stranger.

These are the types of attitudes and behavior expected of a woman. However, some probing indicated that actual behavior varies from couple to couple and also according to the stage of the life cycle they are in. There was unanimous agreement among all women that during the first few years of marriage, that is, until the first pregnancy, life is very difficult for women. Most women enter marriage without knowing the details of the sex act. Many of them have some idea about what it involves by observing animals and listening to gossip, but none of them had witnessed adult men and women having sex. The parents take extra care, and even in households full of people this behavior takes place discreetly and children are not exposed to it. All women are virgins at marriage, and their first experience of sex comes only on the night of the wedding or a few days afterwards. All of them said that the first experience was painful. After some probing, it was clear that it was mainly due to the clumsiness on the part of husbands who themselves have not had much experience. Men generally try to get some experience before marriage with prostitutes and talking about the techniques with friends. But by and large most of them are not adept at it.

Their sex life tends to be very active until the first pregnancy. All women complained about not being allowed to sleep properly night after night nor to visit their *thavaru* frequently or for longer periods of time. The husbands expected them to be there and ready every night, very often several times a night. The first pregnancy is thought of as a big relief by all women as it gives them a chance to visit the *thavaru* for a longer period of time.

Most women related their experience as gradually improving and becoming less and less painful. A few confided that they actually learned to enjoy it and looked forward to it. But for many of them it was a necessary evil that became less bothersome as days passed by. After the birth of the first child, their sex life became less active. For one thing, semen might harm the baby's milk. Therefore, until the baby reaches six months, sex is taboo. If the baby is a girl the taboo might extend only for four months since girls are thought to be hardier than boys. Only in very rare cases do husbands violate these rules. One old woman told me that these rules are violated in these corrupt modern times by indulgent women themselves, not by men. She was very contemptuous towards younger women, who, she believes, have started to enjoy sex, sometimes even as much as men. When I asked what happens if the man is overcome by his strong urges, the answer was that men are very rational when it comes to children. They do not do anything to harm them.

It is customary on the nuptial night before the bride and groom go into the room for the groom's friends to tease him and imply that he is going to make a conquest. Meanwhile, the bride is pitied and consoled and told by the elderly women to lay still on the bed and close her eyes. She is told over and over again not to be afraid and that everything is going to be all right. All conversation with the bride gives the clear impression that she is about to go through some awful, terrible experience.

I told several of these women that I was curious to find out what would happen to a woman who refused to comply with the man's demands. It may be that she has, in fact, some reason to resist. For example, there may be something wrong physiologically or psychologically. They told me that in case of physiological problems, the solution was for the man to marry another woman and no one would accept that there could be a psychological reason for refusing. I was told over and over again that whatever a woman is expected to do, she should do it. Two Brahmin and two Vokkaliga women related to me several incidents of women who refused to comply. In the case of one Brahmin woman her hands and feet used to be tied to the bed post every night until the husband came and had his sex. When she started to scream a cloth was put in her mouth so that no one could hear the scream. In another case (Brahmin) the woman was beaten badly if she refused and gradually she started to comply. In one Vokkaliga case, a wife was beaten to death by her husband as he became fed up with her frequent refusal. In another case the husband left her in the *thavaru*, telling her father that his daughter is of no use to him and got married to another woman. In every case, invariably, sympathies were expressed by all women to the man. All women believed that there is absolutely no excuse for a woman to refuse a man's right.

When I asked whether it is humanly possible for all women to be compliant all the time, I was told that every woman should try. In cases where she cannot, she should learn to convince her man in her own way and make sure it does not become public. A smart woman will learn,

I was told, to handle her man gently and sometimes even get her own way without hurting his pride. It is considered to be very damaging for a woman's reputation if she does not treat her husband properly in bed. Every woman is very afraid of bringing a bad name to her *thavaru* by behaving badly. One woman (Brahmin) told me that her parents warned her on the day she was about to leave for her husband's house that she should have an impeccable character and behave in such a way that will bring credit to her *thavaru*. If she deviated even slightly they would consider her dead, and she would not be allowed to come near their house. The same sentiments were expressed by almost all women in different words. Parents are very conscious of maintaining the reputation of their family and are ready to disown a daughter who brings a bad name. Even though there were no such cases in Musali itself, I was told of instances where the parents refused to see their daughter. It happened in the case of the woman discussed above, whose hands and feet used to be tied every night. She was not allowed to visit her *thavaru* at all, and the woman committed suicide within a year of marriage.[2]

One Vokkaliga woman told me that in cases where the sex life of the man remains active even after several children, the wives encourage the husbands to marry another woman so that they can share the responsibility. This option is helpful in other areas also, because they can share the household chores and farm work. Such an event took place in Musali while I was there. All women think it is wrong to ask a man to go to a prostitute. If a man starts to go to a prostitute, the wife has failed him, and accusing fingers will be pointed at her from every direction, including her *thavaru*.

What happens if the wife enjoys sex and takes the initiative when the husband does not? I was told that in general it should not be done. It is only common sense to keep it under control. There are ways of making the man take the initiative instead of venturing to do it herself. It is always better if he feels that he originated the action. Even if it is in fact not so, a woman can make it look as if it is so. A smart woman, I was told, will have her way but does not make that obvious.[3] One woman in her thirties said that if the husband is in a good mood and trusts the wife completely there is nothing wrong in hinting about her desire. But it should be done tastefully and delicately, never abruptly. The man, it is believed, has a very delicate sense. He is easily offended, and the person who is going to suffer if such a thing happens is the woman. Therefore, one should be very careful not to give any cause for alarm or mistrust.

PREGNANCY AND MOTHERHOOD

When a woman becomes a mother, especially the mother of a son, her status goes up in her new home for having helped perpetuate the family.

As soon as she becomes pregnant, everyone starts to treat her in a special way. She is not allowed to do too much hard work. Special, nutritious meals are given to her. As in other parts of the world, women are believed to have special cravings during pregnancy. According to their wishes, different dishes are given to them. Whether the occurrence of such cravings is real or not, women enjoy receiving special attention for the first time in their life. For precisely these reasons some women look forward to becoming pregnant right after marriage. A special ceremony called *Arathi* is performed for them, to remove the evil eye. As part of the ceremony, pregnant women receive special sweet and salt dishes, fruits, and presents. Many women are invited on this special occasion, and coconut, bananas, betel leaves, betel nuts, and sweets are distributed to them.

The average number of children per woman in this village is approximately four, which is slightly below the national average of 4.6 (Dyson and Crook 1984:38). According to villagers, it was not uncommon in the past for a woman to bear as many as twelve children, in some instances, even up to eighteen. But the mortality rate among children also used to be high. At the present time the mortality rate is going down as medical facilities are becoming more easily available. Many villagers are influenced by the ideas of family planning promoted by the government of India. Nevertheless, there is a strong belief that one should not think of family planning until one has had at least two sons. It is because *Ondu kannu kannalla, obba maga maganalla* (Having one son is as risky as having one eye). In general, the number of children the familes have depends upon whether the first two children were sons.

Most women go to their *thavaru* during the first confinement, from the seventh month of pregnancy until the child is about five months old. The parents give the same special attention to her, and the *Arathi* ceremony is again performed. Most children are born at home, attended by women who are relatives and friends. Occasionally nearby hospitals or health care nurses are used. After childbirth, *Araike* (taking care) is done. Women are kept on a special diet for five months after childbirth and confined indoors to avoid exposure to weather which would ruin the health of both baby and mother. The restrictions on diet and movement are severe in the first three months and are relaxed somewhat in the fourth and fifth months.

These customs are observed by both Brahmins and Vokkaligas. As the Vokkaligas are not very concerned about ritual purity, related rituals are less elaborate than for Brahmins. For example, among Vokkaligas, the woman is confined in a separate room with her baby for ten days after childbirth. She is then given a bath, and all her clothes are washed. From then on she stays in a particular room with the windows closed as the draft is supposed to be harmful for health. Members of the family can touch the baby without fear of pollution. Among Brahmins, however, the woman has to pass through several rituals and baths before she becomes ritually pure. She is most polluting for the first ten days after the birth of the baby. After the bath and a religious ritual, the pollution is reduced. She undergoes similar rituals on the thirtieth day after child-birth. She then becomes pollution free if the baby is a boy, but another ritual on the fortieth day is necessary if the baby is a girl.

After her return from the *thavaru* with the baby, a woman is expected to resume her old routine. Of course, since she has a child to look after, she is excused for not doing everything she was doing before. If the baby is a boy, everyone is happy; if it is a girl, she is accepted grudgingly. If a woman keeps on having girls in succession, she is believed to be of bad stock, and sometimes her husband takes another wife to ensure the continuance of family. The same fate awaits a woman who does not have any children.[4] I came across one case where a second marriage was performed because the first wife did not bear any children for six years after marriage. In another, a woman gave birth to a son only after three daughters.

Having a son and rearing him is considered a great experience by all women. Women with several sons are very proud of themselves. All of the mothers had nothing but the most affectionate things to say about their sons. The faces of these women, which generally are somber and sad, used to light up at the mention of their sons. The feelings are understandable when one realizes the kinds of changes that take place in their status after his arrival. In addition, for many women the son made them feel more at home in their husband's house and he was thought of as a true companion in a place filled with strangers.

OLD AGE

In this village, transition from young adulthood to what is referred to as old age is gradual. There is no recognition of the existence of middle years or mid-life crisis. Old age in this village context is not exactly the same as it is in the urbanized West. The focus here is more on change in status rather than changes in physiology. This is not to suggest that physiological changes have not happened at this time. In fact, because the life expectancy of people in Karnataka is fifty-five for women and fifty-seven for men—against all-India average of fifty-six and fifty-seven for women and men respectively in 1971–75 (ICSSR 1975:144)—one can notice many changes taking place. For example, once women enter their mid-forties, they experience changes such as menopause, graying of hair, reduction in energy level, and gradual farsightedness. People are very mindful of these changes, but they ususally attend more to factors affecting their status in the family, such as the arrival of a daughter-in-law into the house or the birth of a grandchild.

In general, as they grow older women exercise a relatively greater influence on the decison-making process in the family. How much influence a woman has depends upon how competent she is in managing affairs and on whether she has developed a congenial and trusting relationship with her husband. On the other hand, if she does not cater to her husband's wishes or does anything to stain the family prestige, her influence diminishes or at least will not increase.

Among Brahmins, as the arenas of activity for men and women are clearly marked, the influence of women is restricted to the affairs of the house. They play an important role in choosing marital partners for their children and at times those of their relatives. The daughters and daughters-in-law will be under their control. Decisions regarding the running of the house are made by them as well. As they become older they tend to become very religious and spend considerable amounts of time in religious rituals and prayers, while the daughters-in-law carry the burden of household duties under their watchful eye.[5]

In Musali, several Brahmin women have attained this stature and exert considerable influence on decision making. However, this is always done tactfully and behind the scenes. It is mandatory that a woman always projects her husband as being in control even when she has considerable influence. Several women have proved their competence in this arena and therefore enjoy the confidence of their men. In each of these marriages the relationship between the couple is amicable, and the husband trusts the loyalty of his wife to him and to his family. There are other women who have been unable to improve their status in the family, partly because of incompetence, but mostly because they have not been able to develop an amicable relationship with their husbands.

Vokkaliga women also have to prove their competence and develop an amicable relationship with their men to be able to exert greater influence as they grow older. In addition to housework, they work side-by-side with men in the fields and therefore have an effect on both areas. They can actually be completely in control of the household affairs and still influence the decisions of men outside the house. They are usually in control of daughters and daughters-in-law and make decisions on the day-to-day affairs of the home without consulting their husbands. They may also give suggestions on running the family business or maintaining the family farm. Of course, as among Brahmins, they should constantly be mindful of the wishes of their husbands and preserve the status and prestige of the family.

Several Vokkaliga women in Musali are held in considerable respect by their husbands. It is not unusual for these husbands to tell their business partners that the final decision with regard to a particular business deal would be made only after their wives are consulted. The wives are also consulted before making decisions on what to grow, where to grow, and when to grow on the family farm. A few wives are allowed to participate in managing the finances of the family. In all cases the final decisions are made by men but women participate to a significant degree. The women are always discreet and do not flaunt their importance in the family. There are several other families in which the women do not have much influence either within the household or outside. Just as in the case of Brahmins this is often because the women are incompetent or have failed to develop a trusting relationship with their husbands.

WIDOWHOOD

Brahmins

Widowhood is the most dreaded event in a woman's life, as it involves loss of status in the family due to her complete identification with her husband. A woman has a right to maintenance in the husband's family even after his death, but she is usually relegated to a completely marginal status. In addition, in the spiritual context, widows are considered inauspicious, since their widowhood is thought to be the direct result of sins in their past lives. Therefore, all women perform religious ceremonies to ensure long life for their husbands. Despite these prayers husbands do sometimes die before their wives. The widow is then expected to spend the rest of her life trying to atone for her past sins.

The widows themselves are thoroughly convinced that they have sinned in past lives. Otherwise, they would not have been punished by God with the terrible state of widowhood. They live like ascetics, eating only two simple meals a day and never anything after the sun is down. They do not attend any auspicious ceremonies like festivals or life-cycle ceremonies and keep out of sight of everyone during such occasions so that they will not pollute the environment through their inauspicious presence. They comb their hair only once a day and tie it in a knot. They wear a single silver bangle on each wrist, a simple chain around their neck, and simple ear studs. They are not allowed to wear the auspicious red mark on their foreheads, rings on their fingers and toes, or any nose ornaments. They wear simple *sarees* and blouses. They work as hard as they possibly can and knowingly let people take advantage of them as a kind of penance for their past sins. They deny themselves the basic comforts of life, not to mention any luxuries or entertainment. They spend most of their time in prayers to God. Other people perpetuate the situation by constantly reminding them of their sinful past. Most people in the village believe that a widow should consider it a favor if she is allowed to serve them to atone for her past sins.

Widows with children live for them; those without usually pine away and often become neurotic. I encountered one such case in Musali. This woman became a widow after only six months of a marriage which had not been consummated. She has lived the austere life of a widow for the past fifteen years and now everyone in the village considers her crazy and no one talks to her. The reason for this assessment is that she sometimes just sits and talks to herself, unaware of anyone present around her. This conversation with herself can be quite loud and abusive at times. She was twice seen running naked in the streets. She cries at odd times. Some days she demands food after dark, but on others she goes without any food. Some days she takes a bath three or four times, but on others she refuses to bathe and family members have to force one on her, since a bath is mandatory for everyone, especially for a widow. On some days she works from morning till night doing everyone's bidding, but on others she looks so angry and hostile towards everyone that no one has the courage to speak to her.

I tried to talk to this woman several times, but she was unwilling or unable to talk with me. As soon as she saw me coming she used to go inside and refused to come out even to say hello. Finally after several attempts, I succeeded in catching her. I sat next to her and started making small talk. She stared at me for quite awhile and answered in mono-syllables. After a few minutes she just started to cry. I tried to comfort her, thinking that I might have offended her in some way, but it did not help. She was taken inside by the family members. I found out later that she cried for a while and then went to sleep.

There are four other widows in the village; they have children and their lives are not so shattered and full of turmoil, but they make sure that they do not have any personal comforts. They work and live for their children. All of them told me that they eat every day because they have to even though they do not deserve it. The only reason they eat is to get the strength to do the day's work. All of them look sad and depressed most of the time; the only time they are happy is when they talk about their children, especially their sons.

Widows are considered as pollutants, and therefore orthodox people refuse to eat cooked food prepared by them. This is because these women have not gone through the purification ceremony. All widows used to go through this cermony in the past to remove pollution, but nowadays it is not very common though it is sometimes done. Almost all women of my age have witnessed this elaborate, gruesome ceremony. I still remember vividly the feeling of horror I experienced when, as a young girl of about ten years of age, I watched one such ceremony.[6] The woman who went through this process was a close friend of my mother. The tragedy of her husband's death struck and shocked everyone, though it was expected.

Ratna was from a moderately well-to-do family. She was married to an old man whose wife had died leaving no children. Ratna always thought (according to my mother) that it was her bad luck that her parents could not find a suitable match for her. Her parents wanted to leave all their wealth (which was quite substantial by village standards: about five acres of wetland, three acres of garden, and five acres of dry land, some money and jewelry) to their son and were unwilling to spend much on Ratna's marriage so they chose the old man in order to minimize expenses. As may be expected, the marriage was dull and unhappy. Ratna was very beautiful but the husband was old, poor, and ugly. Ratna always felt that she married beneath her but tried to make the best of what she got. Their sexual life from all accounts was unsatisfactory as he was an old man with waning sexual vigor. It was a marriage that was empty for both the partners. Everyone expected the old man to die and leave Ratna to become a young widow, and this is precisely what happened.

When the old man died, a kind of gloom descended on the whole community. Still, everyone was busy making funeral arrangements which had to be done. There are many religious ceremonies that must be performed, starting with the cremation of the body. It is on the tenth day after death that the purification of the widow was ceremoniously done. During the ten days after death, the son (adopted in this case) performed all the ceremonies, and the wife was a silent spectator in the proceedings. On the tenth day, she was made to remove all her bangles, rings, necklace, and the *Kumkum* (sacred red mark) on the forehead. She was no longer allowed to wear clothes of any color except red from that day onwards. The village barber was called in to complete her disfigurement by shaving her head. From that day on, she was not allowed to wear any flowers or perfume. She had to cover her head and wear the *saree* in a way so as to hide her body and make it look as shapeless as possible. The transformation of appearance was tragic and unbelievable. As a last chance, the day before the ceremony, the woman was allowed to wear her finest *saree* and dress herself the way she liked best, complete with jewelry, ornaments, flowers, and perfume. She worshipped the family god for the last time in fine attire.

I still remember Ratna dressed in a green silk *saree* with *butta* (gold finery sprinkled all over) with a large border and a red blouse with *jeri* (gold thread) and large round *kumkum* in the middle of her forehead. Her beautiful long black hair was done in a pigtail curled up behind her head to make a *heralu* (a kind of hair style) with threaded jasmine with green leaves woven in, and her neck was adorned with golden chains. She wore many green bangles between two gold ones on each hand, silver rings on her toes, *muguthi* with *besari* (nose ornaments) on her nose, beautiful white stone inlaid gold ear studs, and a golden belt in the middle of her small waist. She had a gorgeous figure, a beautiful face with a long straight nose, dark brown eyes with long lashes, full red lips, pale flawless cheeks, arched eyebrows, shapely ears and chin, an elegant neck and long fingers bedecked with gold rings. She looked like a goddess. There she was, tears in her eyes, worshipping. All women of the community were with her in her hour of sorrow. My mother especially was crying continuously, as were many other women. Nobody was talking. Men seemed not to involve themselves with all this except for the priest who officiated the ceremony and Ratna's brother who remained at her side most of the time.

The next day this beautiful woman was deliberately, systematically, and ceremoniously turned into an ugly creature clad in red, without a blouse, without any ornaments. Women cried a lot, while men looked on silently. That was the first time I had witnessed such an event and was completely perplexed. Even though I had earlier seen many disfigured widows clad in red, it had not made such an impact on my mind. But suddenly, when I saw this transformation, the emotional turmoil I went through is beyond description. I remember asking my mother why they are removing her beautiful hair which was so long, thick, and shiny; my mother just hushed me and told me not to ask any questions and to go play or do something. She probably did not know what to say. It was quite obvious that she was very unhappy.

Since then there have been several such events that took place in the village which my mother forbid me to witness, as I was asking too many questions. I myself was not very enthusiastic to go through that again anyway and therefore kept away. This one event has remained etched in my memory. As Ratna lived very close to our house, I saw her and talked to her quite frequently. I do not know what went on in her mind, but she became very pensive for a few years and was not talking much with anyone. One day I saw her looking at herself in the mirror, tears streaming from her eyes. As soon as she saw me, she tried to hide the mirror and told me that she was only trying to remove some dust from her eyes. She asked me to promise not to tell anyone that she was looking at herself in the mirror. I could not understand why she was so particular about it. Later I found out that a widow is not supposed to even touch a mirror, let alone look at herself in it. I guess she was afraid of the gossip among people if they heard what she was doing. I learned when I visited the village this time that Ratna had died a few years ago. Even now, her memory haunts me and leaves me sad whenever I think of her.

I asked many women about widowhood and how they felt about what was done to widows. The general comment was that they feel sorry for them but that there is nothing they can do as it is all part of a woman's destiny.

Vokkaligas

The life of a widow among Vokkaligas is not as bleak as among Brahmins. Widowhood does not carry the connotation of inauspiciousness among these people as life is not so ritual ridden as among Brahmins. Widowhood for these women means economic deprivation, especially for those with young children who have to work very hard just to have two meals a day. Women with grown children are generally better off, especially if they have sons. I talked to five widows among the Vokkaligas (there are about ten in the community). They feel very lonely, overworked and underfed. But they do not feel the need to inflict pain on themselves. Vokkaliga widows also believe that it was their own bad luck and the sin of past lives that made them lose their husbands. But a normal, honest, and hardworking life will do to atone for this sin. They do not see any reason for extra punishment. Nevertheless, they are also very depressed and lonely.

Widows are allowed to remarry even though it is not considered very desirable. Lack of virginity reduces their value in the marriage market, and the men who are willing to marry such women are generally poor or deformed in some way, so most widows prefer not to marry at all. This is especially true for women with children since children from the first marriage are not allowed to live with the second husband.

Widows with no children in Musali sometimes take this chance. This second marriage is called *kudike* and is carried out in a very simple way without any elaborate ceremony. The couple go to a temple with close family members like brothers, sisters, and parents and exchange flower garlands. I came across a couple in Musali where the marriage was the second one for the woman. The man had a bad leg which prevented him from working very efficiently in the field. In addition, he was very poor. The woman who married him for the second time was, at the time of marriage, very poor herself and had no children, brothers, sisters, or parents or any close relatives. They had a son, now about ten years old. The husband died of some disease during my stay in the village. The woman was heartbroken at losing a husband for the second time; her son was her life now, and she says she is going to live for him and make sure his life will be better than her own.

The people in the community do not put her down in any way. They understand that she married for the second time because she did not have anyone to call her own in the whole world. Her son by the second marriage is treated just like any other little boy; no stigma was attached to him for being the son of a second marriage as far as I could see. According to villagers, this is not always true because the general tendency is to devalue such children. In this case, it appears that people had taken extra pity on a lonely woman without any kith or kin.

DEATH

"We cry the day a woman is born and the day she is married but we heave a sigh of relief on the day she dies." These sentiments were expressed to me by a Vokkaliga woman in these words. The sigh of relief is to indicate the hope and expectation that she will never again be born a woman, if she has to be reborn at all. These sentiments are shared by both Vokkaliga and Brahmin women. Death for a woman is not thought of as a tragedy since her life itself is perhaps worse. Besides, a woman can be easily replaced. As the saying goes: *Maga sattare manehalu, sose sattare shōbana* (If the son dies, the family is destroyed but if the daughter-in-law dies there will be a wedding).

A woman always hopes that she will die before her husband. Death as a *muthaidē* (a woman with a living husband) assures her journey into heaven. In contrast, only a woman who is condemned is destined to become a widow. Hindus in general believe in rebirth. The goal of one's life is to achieve salvation by escaping the cycle of rebirth. Discharging ones duties in this life diligently is the way one accumulates spiritual merit which eventually leads to salvation. Women try very hard to live up to the ideals of Pativratya and fervently pray that they be not born again, particularly not as women.

Among Brahmins there is a difference in the rituals that are performed for widows and *muthaidēs*. For the death of a widow or a man no festivals are celebrated for one year, nor is the house decorated with greenleaves or flowers, nor are guests entertained. But if a *muthaidē* dies these mourning customs are omitted; her death is not considered a sad occasion; her journey to heaven is assured. Among Vokkaligas, such differentiation is not made; and the ceremonies are not as elaborate as among Brahmins.

However, a woman's death, whether as a *muthaidē* or as a widow, is greatly mourned by her children, because she is cherished by them. There is none so unlucky as a child without a mother. Mother's love is so precious that it cannot be replaced by anything else. Many women explained to me with tears in their eyes how exasperated they felt very frequently in their life and how often they have thought of suicide, but as soon as they looked at the helpless faces of their children and imagined their lot in the hands of a stepmother, they invariably determined to make a go of it. The general feeling was that they should live only as long as their children need them. Most women think that the ideal time for a woman to die is after the children are settled in life, and of course, before her husband. In the village many children without mothers had suffered badly without anyone to take proper care of them. Many women who had lost their own mothers while they were still young told me with great sadness how their life would have been different if only she were alive, because it is only a mother who worries about a daughter and tries her best to make sure that she is married to a good man and into a good family.

Chapter VIII

PATIVRATYA AND WOMEN'S PERSONALITY

In the village of Musali there is an almost one-to-one relationship between the society's cultural values and norms on the one hand and personal normative beliefs of the women on the other. The implicit faith in male superiority and female inferiority is not simply ingrained into the belief system in a passive way: the beliefs color the acquisition of new knowledge and the exposure to new experience. The legitimacy of the system is not only axiomatic to people in Musali; it allows them to describe it as though it should be self-evident to all people. Only out of a deepened appreciation of these fundamental beliefs can one understand the conviction with which women fear that they will not be able to live up to the self-denigrating expectation of the culture. It is indeed difficult to be a Pativrata. One woman told me guiltily that she felt very hungry even before her husband had been fed. This, in the moral context of her life, is a lapse in her character because a good wife never even thinks of, let alone eats, food herself, before her husband has eaten. It is not just a schoolgirl's conception with a heightened moral consciousness. These women think that getting angry at a child just once in awhile is evidence that they will never become perfect wives and mothers. They reiterate that they are not like those great Pativratas but only insignificant mortals.

Women develop an inner conviction regarding the legitimacy of the system as they go through various rituals and ceremonies elaborating the underlying value orientation of this ideology. As Wilson writes, "Rituals reveal values at their deepest level. . . . [M]en express in ritual what moves them most and since the form of expression is conventionalized and obligatory it is the values of the group that are revealed" (Turner 1969:6). Thus the unquestioned faith in the validity of the belief system is celebrated in the form of these rituals. These rituals bring the community together by affirming the shared beliefs. They reaffirm the faith of a given people in the legitimacy of institutionalized relationships (Durkheim 1965:462–76). This is true whether one is referring to rituals relating to pollution and purity (puberty and menstruation), merging of identity (marriage), or depersonalization (widowhood). Women feel as though they are transformed into a new state of being after undergoing these rituals (Turner 1969). They come out of these experiences thoroughly convinced of their physical and spiritual inferiority.

The cultural construction of woman as person is that she is encompassed by man and complementary to him, because she nurtures the man's seed in her womb and delivers his son(s). She thus enables the male line to continue, ensuring the man's immortality. Notions of the auspiciousness and inauspiciousness of woman depend on her relationship to man. Ideally, she is married, with her husband living, *mu-thaide*; this is the most auspicious state. At the other end of the continuum is the widow, who is most inauspicious.

For Hindu women roles are clearly defined and learned through apprenticeship. There is no separation of moral education from other aspects of learning. Girls are systematically prepared to play their adult roles as wives and mothers. Their outlook and attitudes are shaped through the manner of allocation of resources and the kind of attention paid to their needs. They are trained to become docile and compliant.

Instructions in morality and administration of discipline are direct, with no complex techniques of mediation. Behavioral tenets are assimilated naturally. Even the day-to-day behavior is structured through deference customs, constantly reminding women of their subordinate position in society. The socialization practices from infancy to adulthood are geared to nurturing and sustaining a dependent self.

As is evident, the behavioral prescriptions for everyone are considered as irrevocable. The social control is very rigid, and those who deviate from established norms are punished repressively. The coerciveness of moral standards becomes clear when one views it in the context of individual lives. The usual methods of punishment are gossip, ridicule, social disapprobation, or, in extreme cases, social ostracism and physical punishment.

The ideology of Pativratya, by incorporating the basic Hindu values of self-realization, helps perpetuate the partiarchal structure by making the personal goals of a woman fit the structural needs. The system of symbols gets enshrined in the institutional structure. In this context a woman is convinced that she should live through others and for others. She accepts that it is the only way since she is made to believe that she is in possession of a pollutable body and an impulsive mind. She is constantly wary of her actions because she believes that her deeds can harm others.

Perhaps the most invidious form of social control that this ideology imposes upon women is to goad them into claiming moral superiority through self-denigration. The more a woman lowers herself, the more she is praised. The ideal woman is one who looks down upon herself and lives for others. This expectation is taken so seriously that some women put themselves through extreme forms of deprivation, in some cases even self-destruction. The practice of *sati*, the self-immolation of widows, is a good example of the latter. The *satis* actually are the saints among women. At the present time some Brahmin women, especially widows, become so obsessed with this need that they practice various austerities depriving themselves of the most basic bodily needs like food and sleep and continuously indulging themselves in various kinds of worship. They also demand the most exemplary behavior from their wards, namely daughters and daughters-in-law.

In this context, women tend to be very fatalistic and superstitious. This is understandable when one realizes that marriages are arranged and a woman's happiness depends on the kind of household she is married into, the kind of man the husband is, whether she will bear any sons or not, whether she dies before her husband, and whether the children are grown up when she dies. Her happiness always seems to depend on someone else's actions or on chance.

In interpersonal relationships many of these women adopt strategies like crying or fasting to get their own way. While dealing with children they tend to be impulsive; they discipline the children not when they deserve it but when they themselves are in a bad mood. Even in dealings with their adult sons some of them tend to be vulnerable and dependent.

As mentioned before, the ideal woman in the Hindu context is the shy, quiet, retiring, and compliant one, not one who is active and in-quisitive. She is not expected to take active interest in any aspect of life, including the sexual. Trying very hard to live up to these ideals, women become preoccupied with playing their roles correctly. In the process, they lose their inquisitiveness and curiosity.[1]

The belief that women are evil and a burden on men is internalized by the women of Musali. They have low self-esteem and a negative self-image. Most women have little sense of personal worth and think that being a woman is bad in itself. They believe in the cultural devaluation of women's work. They observe the deference customs and all of the self-denigrating rituals relating to menstruation, marriage, and widow-hood without any complaint.

Girls acquire a body image that is dirty and pollutable. As women are believed to be by nature impulsive, untrustworthy, dishonest, and given to exaggeration, women and girls do not take themselves seriously and would rather trust the judgment of men. They become insensitive to their bodily feelings. Adult women and even girls, for example, do not take care of themselves when they are sick as they believe that a woman's body is hardy and not much attention is needed to make it survive. Some adult women go to the extent of saying that even if the sickness becomes worse, it does not really matter. On the other hand, they make a fuss over men and boys when they become sick. Even with regard to taste preferences women take pride in saying that they can eat whatever is available. An important piece of advice given to a new bride is that she should learn to eat whatever the mother-in-law prepares without complaint.[2] Women generally eat whatever is left over after everyone is fed and do not pay any attention to whether it has become cold or whether or not it tastes good.

PATTERNS OF ADAPTATION

Life under this androcentric ideology within a patriarchal social structure becomes tolerable and can even be pleasant, as one woman puts it, if things work out well and if one is lucky. The lives of Brahmin Suma and the Vokkaliga Kittamma illustrate this point (see Appendix A, Case Histories 3 and 43). Despite problems with in-laws for the first several years of years of marriage both women felt that they had no serious problems. There is enough to eat; they both have compassionate and caring husbands, have borne sons, and are content with life. Both willingly observe all of the rules of proper womanhood and are grateful for the good life they have. There are a few such situations in Musali.

Not all women are so lucky. The circumstances of Venki, a Brahmin, and Puttamma, a Vokkaliga, both of whom are widows, are sad indeed (see Appendix A, Case Histories 17 and 38). Both feel that fate has been unkind to them and blame their own past sins for their present predicament. Both had to fend for themselves and care for their families with great difficulty. Instead of earning appreciation they were always criticized for not being docile retiring women. Both of them disapprove of their own behavior and wish that they could live like proper Pativratas should. But they realize that their circumstances do not make allowances for this. They cannot do anything but feel sorry for themselves. There are several women in such a predicament in Musali.

The lives of Shankri, a Brahmin, and Manjamma, a Vokkaliga, are also sad, because even though they work untiringly to please their husbands, the husbands continue to be most inconsiderate. There is frequent wife beating in both families and the women live in terror of their husbands. There are several women who are beaten regularly in Musali (see Appendix A, Case Histories 5 and 45).

Most situations fall in between the extremes described above. Things may not be ideal, but neither are they completely intolerable. The following examples give some idea regarding the range of possibilities. Jani, a Vokkaliga, would rather live in the city where her husband is working but her in-laws insist that she live with them until she learns to mind her manners (see Appendix A, Case History 29). Being the youngest daughter of a well-to-do family, Jani was indulged and is very proud of her family and her looks. She is not a bad person by any means but likes to take life easy and have some fun with her husband. Her husband, even though he wants her to be with him, refuses to interfere with his mother's judgment. Jani realizes that the only way she will get to live with her husband is by pleasing her mother-in-law. She is learning to do it fast.

The life of Shanta, a Brahmin, is interesting. By village standards she has everything a woman could ask for. She has sons who have good education, enough to eat at home, and a husband who is kind and considerate. But Shanta is very unhappy and considers herself very unlucky because she lost her parents when she was twelve years old and was married to a village man rather than one in a city. She follows all the rules of good behavior but always tends to be moody and preoccupied (see Appendix A, Case Hisory 18).

The cases of Lalli, a Brahmin, and Dyavamma, a Vokkaliga, illustrate a different type of problem. Both of these women are considered to be very smart, hardworking wives who take care of their respective families well. The families have prospered since their arrival and both have sons. But both their husbands are not considered to be very hardworking. People make fun of them behind their backs as henpecked husbands. The assessment of neighbors is that without the competent mamagement of the household by their wives the families would not function. The women do not like to be considered bossy and try their best to show their husbands off as competent. But this does not seem to convince the villagers (see Appendix A, Case Histories 12 and 46).

In these instances the women try very hard to uphold family prestige and their own personal reputation with varying degrees of success. In none of these cases is the authority of husbands over wives or the goals and conduct prescribed by the ideology questioned. The patriarchal structure does not allow for the evolution of any alternative goals that are morally equivalent for these women. Therefore even when women deviate from normal behavioral expectations it is usually only a frustrated temper tantrum triggered by the burdens of daily life rather than a reasoned dissent. Such people are brought back in line and are made to realize the error of their ways. Even when it is clear that the ideological context allows for inhuman treatment of women, it is dismissed as due to situational exigencies and particular personal failures.

There is no scope for the emergence of organized resistance under these conditions. To begin with, the structural context of women's lives is such that it does not allow for development of separate identities as individual women. They are continuously pushed to become part of the group and lose their individuality. The system of arranged marriage and the ideal characteristics stressed in a woman—shyness and quiet compliance—signify the subordination of individual needs to the objective of group cohesion. Achievement of this objective is gained through the encouragement of an intensely shared life. The ideal of Pativratya clearly enunciates that a woman should live *through* others and *for* others. When exposed to new ideas and new ways of doing things, these are automatically rejected as irrelevant and inapplicable to their own situation.

In this context, the only membership group for women is their kinship group. If women meet other people outside the house at all, the ones they meet belong to their own caste and are often relatives. There are no other groups available to them; this unavailability greatly reduces the scope for developing their individuality by participating in several groups (Levine 1971:251–93).

EXCEPTIONS

A few women in the village do not fit exactly into the pattern described above. They are three women from the Brahmin caste—Shami, Sharada, and Jaya—and two women from the Vokkagliga caste—Jayamma and Thayamma. The attitudes and behaviors of these women are significantly different from the general pattern. All of them look optimistically toward the future and are not overly concerned with bad aspects of being women. They are emotionally more secure and have a positive self-image. They tend to blame the village environment for most of the trouble women face, rather than blame their own fate. They do not consider that being a woman is intrinsically bad (see Appendix A, Case Histories 4, 9, 10, 35, and 37).

A careful look into the background characteristics and life-style of these women reveals an interesting pattern. It appears that some opportunities for autonomy and self-direction are open to these women. The avenues are different for women of different castes. Older Vokkaliga women are relieved of the drudgery of daily housework with the arrival of daughters-in-law. And their role as managers of household and consultants in business/farming matters seems to enhance their self-image. This is not to suggest that all older Vokkaliga women enjoy these privileges in fact. But it does indicate that structurally conducive conditions are available for women at this age if they are competent to make use of them. In addition, these women have to be very conscious of the limits and work carefully within them. Under no circumstances can they make their husbands look bad and still be treated with respect themselves. For older Brahmin women such opportunities are not available since women are restricted to work within the house only. They do have an opportunity to control and direct daughters and daughters-in-law, but they are never completely relieved of housework because adherence to the notion of purity leads to their not relinquishing the responsibility for cooking. The life-style of Brahmin women does not change very significantly as they get older in the same way it happens to Vokkaliga women. Brahmin women cannot even relax their adherence to deference customs as it is done among older Vokkaliga women, since it is considered a mark of good breeding.

The three Brahmin women mentioned above live in a nuclear family context which gives them relatively more autonomy. In addition, they are also exposed to new ideas regarding intersex relationships through education and frequent contact with urban areas. Since the husbands in these families are more accommodating, the women have been able to exert their influence within the family and have relatively more control

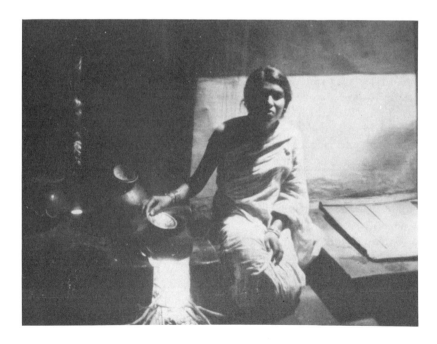

A VOKKALIGA WOMAN PAUSES IN HER KITCHEN.

over their own lives. This is not to suggest that these women are allowed to flaunt their influence in front of people but they can discreetly organize their lives within the family the way they like it. Such a situation has helped these women to develop a more positive sense of self and a positive outlook toward life. Such opportunity for education and frequent exposure to urban areas seem not to be open for Vokkaliga women of this village in general.

SOLIDARITY AMONG WOMEN

The existing structural constraints are such that they prevent development of solidarity among women to protest against the system. Strict social distance is maintained between women of different castes, since castes are hierarchially arranged and there is residential separation on the basis of caste. Brahmin women consider themselves superior in terms of ritual purity, because of their association with Brahmin men. Their life-style also is thought to be more sophisticated because they adhere to a vegetarian diet and work only within the home. They in general are economically better off. Vokkaliga women by and large accept this claim of superiority by Brahmin women. Under these circumstances interaction between women of different castes is virtually nonexistent. The only types of interaction that are allowed to exist are when Vokkaliga women sell various commodities to Brahmin women or when the Vokkaliga women/girls work for the Brahmin women as domestic help.

Women in both castes are governed by the ideology of Pativratya and live in the patriarchal familial context yet they are not conscious of the similarities in the condition of their lives but continually emphasize the differences. Neither is there any scope for development of solidarity among women within each caste because of other structural constraints.

In general mothers and daughters are emotionally very close to each other. The daughter learns from her mother how to cope with a demanding husband, a nagging mother-in-law, and a tale-telling sister-in-law. She also learns how to lower herself, suffer silently, wait patiently— in short, to withstand any onslaught without complaint. She learns all the deference customs that are signs of good breeding. A daughter is often told that if she wishes to retain the privilege of visiting her *thavaru* she should practice all the principles of proper womanhood imparted to her. Mothers thus are also the agents of this patriarchal society who make sure tradition is kept up. A daughter's deviation from the norms reflects on the mother, thereby destroying her reputation.

Mothers make it a point to explain to their daughters very early in life that they should never expect to be treated as special because women are just not special. This is not to indicate that they do not love their daughters. It is precisely because they love them that they teach them how to lower their expectations and learn to cope with life the way it is.[3] The mother knows *Hennina balu kanneeru* (A woman's life is filled with tears). A good mother's role is to teach her daughter the way life is and help her make the best adjustment possible. Mother and daughter get along well as soon as the daughter understands these things. Mothers feel proud of their daughters when they become docile, nurturant, self-effacing, and self-sacrificing.

A mother of a young Brahmin widow in Musali was glowing with pride when she described to me how her daughter has become almost a complete recluse and is practicing various forms of self-discipline by avoiding all the pleasures of life. She eats only twice a day, visits no one, attends no marriages or festivals, and does not wear any good clothes. The mother explained how her daughter just lives for her son and is looking forward to the day her son is well settled in life. She confided in me that her daughter may not even want to live once she has discharged her responsibilities. The mother herself had given up many pleasures just to feel closer to her daughter. They often got together to experience the sorrow. The mother was contemptuous of widows who laughed aloud, went to movies, and attended festivities unashamedly. I asked her whether she feels sorry for her daughter who did not experience any of the pleasures of life. Her reply was that she is not destined to as she must pay for her past sins.

In spite of a strong emotional bond, the interests of mothers and daughters do not coincide. It is in the interest of the daughter to take as much dowry as she can to elevate her position in her husband's family. But it is in the interest of the mother not to allow that to happen but instead to save as much as possible for her son. It is in her personal interest to keep her son wealthy and happy, because it is with him that she spends her lifetime.

Mothers sacrifice the interests of their daughters for the sake of their sons and expect the daughters to understand and sympathize with them. There were several cases in Musali where the daughters were married off to poor families because the parents did not want to deprive their son of a good living by spending too much money for the marriage. Even in day-to-day life mothers actively encourage their daughters to be self-sacrificing and put their interests behind those of their brothers.

In the case of mother-in-law and daughter-in-law, one would expect that their interests would coincide since they both share the same household and are part of the same family. Instead there is much rivalry and competition between the two of them. The antagonism between successive generations of mothers-in-law and daughters-in-law is well documented. The ideology of Pativratya, by promoting a hierarchical relationship between husband and wife, does not provide conditions that would lead to the development of an emotionally satisifying companionate conjugal bond. Since daughters are temporary members of the family, mothers tend to depend on their sons for emotional comfort. The mother-son bond in the family tends to be more emotionally charged than any other because of this special relationship. The marginal position women occupy in their husband's family is improved to full-fledged membership of the family after the birth of at least one son. In this sense, sons are their mother's saviors, and mothers are grateful for this. Because of the emotional comfort sons bring to them, mothers are loath to share their sons with daughters-in-law though they accept it as inevitable. They feel a strong sense of loyalty to their sons and do everything in their power to promote their interests. One important way such loyalty is shown is by making sure that daughters-in-law serve the interests of their sons by being dutiful wives. Thus mothers-in-law actively work toward maintaining daughters-in-law in a subordinate position. The structural arrangements are such that the mothers are co-opted into the patriarchal family and are made to serve its interests.

Women in general believe their loyalty is owed to the men who are in positions of power and privilege. Being accepted and cherished by them is considered a blessing. Women compete with each other for the favor of men, and whenever there is a conflict of interest they betray each other. They also punish each other whenever there is any deviation from expected conduct. The end result is that women work toward maintaining the partiarchal structure rather than toward its erosion.

Chapter IX

PATIVRATYA AND THE HINDU WOMAN'S DESTINY

This book focuses attention on the impact of the androcentric ideology of Pativratya on women's lives. By elaborating on the philosophical underpinnings and the beliefs regarding the nature of men and women it is based on, it shows how women's dependent position on men is legitimized, how the ideology manipulates the motivational structure of women to accept their position as underlings of men, and how it strips them of the willpower necessary for self-reliance and personal growth. It also shows how the ideology, which is built into the patriarchal social structure, determines the social processes that shape women's destiny. The structural context of women's lives is such that they not only tolerate their position as heirs to an unequal opportunity structure—they become active agents in transmitting that heritage to the next generation. By accomplishing these objectives this book has answered questions posed earlier—how and why do women accept their position silently and men of all castes consider this state of affairs appropriate?

In this chapter, using the insights provided, attempts are made to find answers to the other two questions: Why is there a remarkable stability in women's status over time? and Why, in spite of well-intended efforts on the part of the enlightened leadership, has not the plight of Hindu women changed significantly in contemporary India? A brief look at the future prospects for women's destiny is taken, as well.

PATIVRATYA THROUGH HISTORY

The ideals and images that inspire women, their general role expectations, and the overall status of women in Indian society have remained
remarkably stable over time. Historical studies in general have focused
mainly on the upper castes; nevertheless, the same ideals and expectations have filtered into the consciousness of lower castes. The structural
conditions in which women have lived all through the ages have in
general been similar in both upper and lower castes (Sengupta 1974;
Thomas 1964).

The society has always been patriarchal and the family structure
patriarchal, patrilineal, and patrilocal[1]; marriages were arranged, women
did not have freedom of movement or the right to inherit property,[2] and
the cherished ideals of women were the same as they are now, namely
Pativratya.[3] The world of women was always different from that of men,
as society was structured to promote and sustain male superiority. Not
only women's self-fulfillment but also their salvation were in living in the
world of women to maintain the world of men. The belief in the woman's
dual nature and the pollutability of her body were prevalent. The dominant pattern of orientation toward women was reverence toward the
mother and control of the wife. Widowhood was considered inauspicious, virginity before marriage was mandatory, and remarriage was disapproved.[4]

These observations hold up through history except for a short period
during the age of the Vedas, approximately 2500 B.C. to 1500 B.C.. There
is evidence to show that during this time, even though arranged marriage
was the general pattern, free choice of mate was not entirely disapproved.
Women were still denied the right to inherit property, yet they were
given educational opportunities. There was also flexibility in terms of
freedom of movement, opportunity for divorce, and remarriage. Women
were still expected to be inspired by the ideal of Pativratya and were
encouraged to abide by its tenets. Nevertheless, it appears that to achieve
salvation independent means were not completely denied. This can be
deduced from instances where women had become well versed in the
Vedas and Upanishads and led a spiritual life on their own. They were
also allowed to indulge in discussion and dialogue with men as equals,
exploring the nature of the soul and its destiny. Some women also composed Vedic hymns. All of this suggests that while Pativratya was expected to be an ideal for women, other options were not entirely closed
(Upadhyaya 1974: 157, 158; Sengupta 1974: 42–52).

One possible explanation for such a sociocultural milieu during the
period of the Vedas could be that the social structure was not yet rigidly
set in the new country. The Aryans had only recently arrived from far-
off lands. Even though they had brought ideals and images of proper

living from their homeland, these must have taken time to get established. There was scope for individual innovation and interpretation of cherished ideals. For example, as explained in *The Mahabharata*, a woman can be a good wife and mother even if she is learned (Roy n.d.: Vanaparva). Learning and proficiency in the arts, which do not help much in discharging wifely duties, are acceptable as long as they do not interfere with such duties.

When the initial period of confrontation with the natives was over and people became used to the new land, life became settled and systematic. Division of labor and specialization of occupations led to rigid stratification of the social structure. The caste system became entrenched and crystallized, and thus the position of women also. Defining the nature of intercaste relationships and defining woman's position went hand-in-hand; subordination of women and their commodification were a necessary part of defining caste hierarchy and perpetuation of hierarchical relationships. Though women's ability to achieve was never questioned, the wisdom of investing time and energy into something irrelevant for their life goal was.[5] Instead, women should be kept happy within the confines of the home, with material needs and comforts taken care of. According to Manu's laws, women should be respected as mothers, and noble female qualities, like gentleness and unselfishness, praised and cultivated (Buhler 1886: Ch. X, 1–17).

As time passed under these strictures, women became ignorant and superstitious and consequently were not considered as deserving of respect as individuals. Motherhood as a principle was worshipped ritualistically. The mother-son bond continued to be important as the son was viewed as a savior by mothers. By the time Manu's laws were written (about 400 B.C.), the position of women was rigidly set. According to Manu's dictum women were destined to be dependent on men (Buhler 1886: Ch. V, v. 148). Women have continued to lead such a life for centuries.

There is no suggestion of any protest against this system through these years. Even during the times when protest movements against the rigid and inegalitarian caste system became widespread no one asked fundamental questions about the status of women.[6] Many social reformers questioned the unkind treatment of women and appealed to the better sense of men. The few women who protested did not question male superiority or demand equal rights for women. They tried to legitimize other means of salvation for women outside of marriage. For example, devotee Akkamahadavi spent her lifetime being totally devoted to her personal god Shiva and devotee Meera did likewise with her personal god Krishna. The strategy followed was to consider God, whether it be Shiva or Krishna, as one's husband and lead a life devoted to that particular deity.[7]

Through history the day-to-day life of women within the constraints of a strict patriarchal structure was at times tolerable and at others filled with misery. The conditions varied according to overall changes in society and the concerns of men in positions of power. Around 1500 B.C., the time when Aryan invaders successfully dominated the native Dravidians, there was a period of consolidation of power. One way such a consolidation took place was that the Aryans took Dravidian women as additional wives. In general the Aryan wife remained the senior wife, thereby retaining her symbolic status of importance in the marriage. But the introduction of the Dravidian wives into the household deprived the Aryan wife of exclusive influence over her husband. In addition, freedom of movement for wives in general, and for the Aryan wife in particular—to protect her from exploitation by Dravidian men—came into effect (Altekar 1956: 1–33, 345). During the period of the Guptas, from the fourth century B.C. to the seventh century A.D., on the other hand, there was prosperity in the land and stability in political climate. Then women were allowed to cultivate the arts like music and dance (Sengupta 1974: 80–87). After the Muslim invasion around 1100 A.D., the lot of women again worsened because the environment was considered to be hostile. There was further curtailment on the freedom of movement as *purdah* was widely practiced and *sati* widespread. Education for women became unpopular as well (Ibid.: 105–8).

During the British rule in India (eighteenth to mid-twentieth centuries) there were not many significant changes. By-and-large the British maintained a hands-off policy regarding the socioreligious customs of the natives, but many Hindu reformers, influenced by Western liberalism, persuaded the British rulers to enact laws to improve the living conditions of women. These laws prohibited the custom of *sati*, female infanticide, and child marriage and promoted widow remarriage. Even though there were many problems with regard to implementation of these laws, the dedication of many Hindu reformers—most of them men—brought some relief to the lives of many women (Asthana 1974: 24–39).

During the campaign to obtain independence from British domination women participated in large numbers. By all accounts the contributions women made during this struggle were substantial and impressive. Nevertheless, most women took great pains to point out that they were primarily wives and mothers. They did what they did only because their help was needed by their men. In Musali, for example, women voted according to the instructions given by their men. Women often tried to integrate their roles in the national liberation movement with their wife/mother position (Pearson 1982). Even Indira Gandhi is pictured as *Durga mata* protecting her children and helping them to prosper (Jacobson and Wadley 1977: 132).

PATIVRATYA IN CONTEMPORARY INDIA

The constitution of free India guarantees equality for women in every aspect of life. For the first time in history the political will to meaningfully alter the destiny of women has resulted in enshrining these rights in a sacred document (ICSSR 1975: 1–6). A number of laws have been passed toward this end. These laws address the issues related to inheritance of property, marriage, divorce and custody of children, education, employment, and political participation, to name a few. Even though the intent of the enlightened leadership is achievement of equality for women, many of these laws have many loopholes. For example, daughters do not have equal access to property in all parts of the country since certain aspects of customary law have been retained. Women do not have equal matrimonial rights, and the grounds of divorce vary between the sexes (ICSSR 1975: 46–54; de Souza 1975: 96–104). In addition, most of the laws have not been implemented effectively to bring about changes. The 1961 law outlawing dowry, for example, has not made any difference, and the custom is still very widespread and affects the lives of women.

These laws were passed against tremendous odds since the conservative elements in the country were firmly opposed to them. The difficulties that then-Prime Minister Nehru encountered with members of his own (Congress) party and many opinion leaders in the country as he endeavored to steer the laws through the parliament are well documented. A significant core of enlightened leadership had to contend with conservative forces which were generally quite vocal and influential. The passage of these laws against such formidable opposition is viewed as the single most significant achievement of the Nehru era (Nanda 1976: 87–98).

Industrialization and urbanization have opened up white-collar and professional occupations which many educated women in urban areas now fill. But the general rate of women's participation in the workforce is declining. In rural areas where the bulk of the population resides the unemployment rate of women is going up (ICCSR 1975: 65–67; Lebra et al. 1984: 288). Lack of training and illiteracy are the major reasons for women being edged out of the labor market. Many studies have shown that modernization does not necessarily mean better choices for women; instead it can actually lower their status. Because modernization requires new skills and expertise, only those who get a chance to upgrade their skills and expertise benefit, and women are not getting these opportunities. Skilled jobs usually go to men, just as do the managerial ones. In the construction industry, for example, contractors and supervisors are usually men (Lebra et al. 1984: 292–93).

Women do not move from place to place as men do in search of better jobs because of the stigma attached to single women and women living alone. If they flaunt this social taboo women can become targets of harassment and social ostracism. If they suffer from discrimination on the job, women do not have any option but to accept whatever is available. In addition, there is a high dropout rate among professional women in the urban areas in the field of medicine, nursing, and teaching. Even though there is great need for their services in the rural areas, since women prefer to be treated and taught by women, these urban women are reluctant to move to rural areas (ICSSR 1975: 93; Lebra et al. 1984: 113–14). Under these circumstances, women's commitment to jobs and professions is also often questioned by employers, as indicated by statements such as: "Women are still apologetic about working." "They are not proud of their accomplishments as they should be. They are always making excuses for going out to work" (Lebra et al. 1984: 112).

Equal educational opportunities are open for women, according to the law. The literacy rate among women is increasing, but there is great variation between states, with Kerala having the highest (51 percent) and the lowest (8 percent) in Rajasthan. There is also a rural-urban difference, with 13 percent and 41 percent respectively. The average literacy rate is about 19 percent. The number of girls attending school is gradually increasing, but this is much more likely in urban areas than in rural ones. The dropout rate is much higher among girls than boys. Besides the ratio of female to male students declines dramatically as one moves up the educational ladder (ICSSR 1975: 90–91).

Opportunities for professional training, especially in teaching and medicine, have been available for women even though they are not visible in more prestigious and economically lucrative specialties such as surgery and law (Lebra et al. 1984: 149; ICSSR 1975: 77; Research Unit on Women's Studies 1975: 29).

The number of girls attending colleges is steadily increasing. But, as Goldstein (1972: 60) points out, many female students think that colleges are places one spends time until one gets married. The college environment has not done much to stir their imagination, challenge their intellect, or inform them of their rights and duties. Women's education frequently is not taken seriously. In some colleges, a separate curriculum is prescribed for males and females, with the latter being trained to become efficient home makers (ICSSR 1975: 88–99). Such strategy facilitates maintenance of the status quo rather than promoting equality between the sexes. The recommendation of *Status of Women Report* is to make a uniform curriculum accessible to both males and females and integrate the issue of equality in the curriculum (ICSSR 1975: 98–99).

The laws of the land provide for equal participation of women in the political processes. Women have participated mainly as voters. There has not been a substantial number of women representatives in national or state assemblies—only 4.2 percent in the former and 2.7 percent in the latter (ICSSR 1975: 103–15). The percentage of women candidates has been declining since 1962. This does not augur well for the future of women. As one politician puts it, "If the generation of women from the freedom movement is vanishing, a new generation of politically conscious women dedicated and actively inspired to change this society into an egalitarian one is not coming up" (Lebra et al. 1984: 226).

The few women in the parliament and state assemblies have not been very effective in improving on the status of women. First of all, their numbers are small. Besides the majority of the female politicians are from upper-middle- and upper-class families who have been involved in politics over time ((Lebra et al. 1984: 221–27). Born into privilege, they have achieved their personal goals with the support of family members. Their elite life-style colors their outlook. In general they work within the system, stress the responsibilities of citizenship, and advocate voluntary social service for the improvement of women (Lebra et. al 1984: 227–34).

The accepted goals of planned national development in contemporary India are maximum production, full employment, economic equality, and social justice for all, which includes women. But when one looks at the most basic of human needs—personal health and welfare—women in general do not fare well. This is especially true in rural areas. The sex ratio is steadily declining, from 972 females per 1000 males in 1901 to 930 females per 1000 males in 1971. The mortality rate is consistently higher for females, especially in the age group birth-to-four and fifteen-to-thirty-four. After careful scrutiny, the *Status of Women Report* states that the cause for declining sex ratio is systematic neglect of women and girls (ICSSR 1975: 118–22). They suffer from malnutrition as well as underutilization of preventative and curative health services.

These examples, and the investigations they represent, clearly indicate that in spite of best intentions on the part of the enlightened leadership in contemporary India significant changes have not taken place in women's lives. The reason for this state of affairs becomes clear when one examines the implications of the ideology of Pativratya for Hindu women's lives in contemporary India. Agnew (1979: 132–44) shows how the elite women who are supposed to be the opinion leaders for the masses are strictly ruled by the ideology of Pativratya. Kapur (1970: 399–415) commenting on the determining factors of marital adjustment for married women in the productive labor force, states that only those marriages where women willingly make adjustments are considered harmonious. She uses findings from her own study as well as those of others to support this argument. The marriage manuals exhort the wife to be docile and compliant (Niranjana 1977). The divine story recitals heard mostly by women all through the year but especially during festival seasons are obsessed with the theme of Pativratya. The popular literature and the entertainment media such as movies constantly dwell on the theme of selfless, self-sacrificing wife/mother.

The prospects for change for the status of women under these circumstances are bleak indeed. It is clear that implementation of the existing laws as well as introduction of new laws can only come about if the women who would be the direct beneficiaries demand it. But most women are not aware of these laws (Luschinsky 1963). Even when a few women become aware of them, they are reluctant to press forward against tremendous odds existing in their life circumstances. We have to understand clearly the kinds of rigid constraints women experience in their daily lives to explain why such demands are not forthcoming.

Women are exclusively responsible for reproductive labor (housework, daily maintenance of family members, and the bearing and rearing of children) which is neither remunerated in monetary terms nor recognized as a contribution since it is defined as their duty. Women are defined as dependents on their husbands. Husbands are held responsible for their wives' economic well-being since wives are appropriated as persons by husbands in this ideological context. Such a situation leads to gender stereotyping of productive and reproductive labor; men provide for the former and women for the latter.

The women who do participate in the productive labor force are defined as secondary earners, working only to supplement the husband's earning when and if needed. Such a stance leads to discriminatory practices on the part of employers, whether in terms of providing job opportunities for women, job training, or pay equity with men. Beneria and Sen (1981: 283) note that in a context where ". . . patriarchal vision of the male wage as the main source of family income, women's wages (then) are viewed as complementary rather than primary which explains women's willingness to work for a lower wage and helps to explain why women's wages often remain barely 50% of male wages in cases where women's productivity is as high if not higher than men's." If a woman does obtain a job, she is probably supplanting a man who needs to support a family. In Musali the few women who worked for wages outside the home, either because they were widows or because their labor contribution was needed to make ends meet, were paid as little as 60 percent of what men earned for the same or similar work, and they were the first to be laid off when this was necessary. Such situations are documented by many other studies in different parts of the Indian subcontinent (Safa and Leacock 1981; Jain 1980; Lebra et al. 1984).

When women are involved in productive labor, it is considered only as an extension of their wife/mother role. Husbands reserve the right not only to allow their wives to work but also to appropriate their earnings. This often happened in Musali, particularly to the wages the Vokkaliga women made outside the home or the money they earned through handicrafts or the curing of various agricultural produce. Jain (1980: 34) documents similar problems in the urban areas. In addition, particularly for Brahmin women, their seclusion within the house has resulted in the exploitation of their labor. The middlemen make money through the work of women. The handicrafts they make bring them a fraction of the market price, and the curing of various agicultural produce done within the home brings in far less than the minimum wage given workers in the "productive" labor force. Mies (1982) observes a similar situation among the lacemakers of Narsapur. Her conclusion regarding the relationship between productive and reproductive labor leading to exploitation of women is very instructive. She argues cogently that the system of seclusion of women and the definition of all their work as being an extension of the housewife role leads not only to lower wages for women under unhealthy conditions but also their meek acceptance of such a situation. As she writes, "The men not only control certain means of production, but also the means of reproduction, namely their women. Domestication of women means nothing but that a man is able to control all productive and reproductive functions of a woman" (p. 112).

In this ideological context employers are loath to invest in the career advancement of women since they are thought of as lacking any long-term commitment. The kinds of jobs women get are most often temporary and dead end, with less earning potential than their male counterparts. In addition, women have to face a "double bind" when they participate in the productive labor force because reproductive labor has a stigma of women's work attached to it and is therefore devalued. Men refuse to take part in such devalued labor even when they need women's earnings. In this ideological context the expectations are such that a woman cannot but carry this double burden if she is to maintain her reputation as a good wife. A woman's prestige is at stake if she does not perform her reproductive labor properly. Faced with such pressures and finding it impossible to cope, some women may quit their paying jobs, thereby reinforcing the stereotype that women do not have serious commitment to work outside the home. This occurs frequently when a woman has a new baby, since support services are seldom available (Jain 1980).

Evidence from many sources is accumulating that for women to be the equals of men in the larger society they have to be their equals within the home. Unless the reproductive and productive roles in society are integrated and men and women share work in both spheres, equality for women will remain an illusion. This conclusion is clearly stated by Kelly: "[C]ulture is an important factor when considering women's social status.... [T]he part that culture plays in facilitating or preventing the participation of women in remunerated labor, their organization in the workplace and their transformation into dependent housewives ... are the various ways in which women are socially controlled and their labor appropriated both within the household and in the market place" (1981: 276).

The commitment to Pativratya by both men and women has led to toleration of the kind of treatment women get within the home and in the labor market. Even if women think it is unfair, more often than not there is not much they can do about it. Besides, they are scattered in individual families and often are not allowed to go out on their own (Mies 1982). Women are not organized to gain strength in unity and to find words to voice their concerns. Many labor organizers find it difficult to organize women. First of all women are not used to belonging to extrafamilial associations. Historically they have been submerged in the family, especially so in the case of upper-caste women. Getting them out of the home and getting them to belong to these associations has been most difficult. In addition, women are overworked and have neither the time nor the energy to participate in these activities after completing their double shift. Jain (1980: 31) shows the kinds of problems women face at home that prevent them from organizing. She argues that women can organize successfully only when the problems they face at home are also addressed.

In the present ideological context the permission of husbands for women's involvement outside the home is considered mandatory (Madan 1976; Mazumdar 1976). Even during the struggle for independence women would come out of the home to participate in any activity only with the support of their men. The same was true for the women who became members of the Panchayat in Musali. Women take great pains to point out that they are primarily wives and mothers and have taken a little time off to come out of the home only because their help was needed by their men.

In addition, through the influence of Pativratya women have been silenced by stressing the qualities of docility, meekness, selflessness, and self-sacrifice and therefore cannot object to the kind of treatment they get either within or outside the home. If being respectable means being meek and docile, speaking out and complaining about situations is dangerous. If suffering silently is considered one of the moral strengths of women, it is not proper to protest. *Women are socialized to internalize these expectations*. In addition, learning to believe that women are less deserving than men because they are women effectively weakens the will to argue on one's own behalf. Even in middle-class urban families, as Kapur (1970: 432–33) shows, it is those marriages where women play the traditional role that are conflict free. Women, whether urban or rural, play an active role only in arenas considered internal to the family (Conklin 1979). Under such circumstances women become incapable of the assertive behavior which is required for effective participation in the productive labor market. The unquestioned acceptance of Pativratya leads to the development of a personality characterized by compliance, docility, and low self-esteem which are not conducive for organized resistance against unequal treatment.

Women are also effectively silenced by invoking patriotic and ethnocentric attitudes. It is argued that by being assertive and individualistic Indian women will be abandoning the Hindu ideal of womanhood and aping the Western woman who is not only unpatriotic but also immoral. Kelly shows that women are put in a moral dilemma by invoking such conflicting loyalties: "[W]omen's status and participation in economic and political affairs cannot be fully appreciated without consideration of the overall socioeconomic reality of a nation or a country. Moreover, to bolster their opposition to Western and imperialistic influences, nationalist struggles often make use of traditional ideologies that are deleterious to women's status. In short, progressive political positions about development frequently confront irreconcilable alternatives" (1981:274).

The effect of Pativratya on the treatment of daughters in terms of personal well-being and the provision of an opportunity structure for personal growth and economic benefit is quite strong. Most parents consider daughters a burden and an inconvenience. Preference for sons over daughters is widespread, and sons are intrinsically more important. Even the slogans used in family planning campaigns by the government of India reinforce the status of the male child (Rao 1983: 164). There is evidence to suggest the prevalence of neglect of female children (Miller 1981). In Musali as well, daughters were not as well cared for, especially when they were sick.

According to Pativratya, marriage is a must for all women. Belief in the pollutability of the female body makes it necessary that marriages be arranged. Arrangement of a marriage is an onerous task since parents are required to be solicitous towards the groom and his people. Besides marriage is expensive since it often involves dowry. Marriage expense is the major investment parents make in a daughter's future. More often than not daughters are denied their rightful share in the parental property in defiance of the law because, it is argued, the marriage expenditure more than compensates for the denial of property. In this book there is ample evidence that, even when arranging a marriage, some parents are reluctant to spend too much which leads to making marriage alliances that are not in the daughters' best interest. Investing too much in a daughter's education is often considered unwise; it increases the cost of marriage since one has to find a bridegroom who is better educated than the bride. Dowry increases proportionately with the level of education of the groom. In general, the better the match one looks for, the more one has to spend. In addition, parents consider it uneconomical to invest in a daughter's education because the contribution will not return to the parental family since she is not a permanent member (ICSSR 1975: 95; Research Unit on Women's Studies 1975: 28–29). The patrilocal residence pattern and the system of patrilineage requires that girls become part of their husband's family after marriage. Thus the daughter moves from a marginal status in the parental home to a marginal status in the husband's home until a son is born.

Once a son is born, a woman's status dramatically changes, and she does become a full-fledged member of her husband's family. Her influence within the family in general and her control over her daughter(s) and daughter(s)-in-law in particular becomes more significant. Mothers relish their power and influence within the family. Such a feeling is understandable; for the first time in her life she is in charge rather than required to toe a line drawn by someone else. But it is important to understand clearly that she is accorded status and power within the family only to serve the interests of her husband and his family. What this means in concrete terms is that she trains her daughter to become a docile compliant woman fit to become a Pativrata and monitors the behavior of her daughter(s)-in-law vigilantly to make sure that she does not veer away from the tenets of this ideology. Thus the subordinate position of women is passed on from one generation to the next. The tragic irony of it all is that women are co-opted into the patriarchal family to become willing and active participants in perpetuating their own subordination.

A LOOK INTO THE FUTURE

Women's claim for equality has legitimacy in contemporary India since it is enshrined in the Constitution. Besides, the passage of various laws signifies the clear intent of the enlightened leadership to make it a reality. Nevertheless it appears that unless women become aware of their rights and demand that they be accorded those rights there is no possibility of any real change.

Historically women have been singularly incapable of making such demands. Any change in women's life circumstances has come about through the efforts of many men of good will and compassion. The women's liberation movement until very recently has not been militant enough to draw attention to the plight of women. It more often than not focuses attention on improving educational opportunities for women and elevating the status of downtrodden women through voluntary social work. Its appeals are made to the better sense of those in positions of power, and it exhorts people to have compassion towards women suffering from various kinds of oppression (Asthana 1974: 24–39; Nanda 1975: 41–66).

In recent years, especially in the 1960s and the 1970s, many new associations have sprung up which are explicitly militant and demand equality for women. There is a women's liberation movement in India sharing the same goals and aspirations of this worldwide movement

(Everett 1981; Omvedt 1980; Research Unit on Women's Studies 1975). It is true that the movement does suffer from factionalism. Caste, class, language, and regional barriers, among others, keep the various groups apart. Each of these groups is working from its own vantage point, addressing the issues of concern of its membership. Some of the issues addressed are: to promote education of women, to help women protect themselves as consumers from the exploitation of unscrupulous merchants, to protect women from the tyranny of dowry, to improve conditions in the workplace and insure better pay, to organize urban poor and landless laborers to improve their lot, to protect women from violence within the home and in the streets, and to protect against pornography and commodification of women. The strategies followed include dissemination of information regarding the rights of women through speeches and in pamphlets, newspaper articles, magazines, and journals. Attempts are made to draw the attention of media and those in positions of power through demonstrations of various types and by organizing conferences and symposia (Omvedt 1980; Everett 1981; Davies 1983: 3–8, 197–214, 249–352; Research Unit on Women's Studies 1975: 79–81; Asthana 1974: 84–108; Kishwar and Vanita 1986).

Those women who are forming these associations are learning to speak in their own behalf. Many of them are gaining courage and developing convictions of their own. Instead of accepting unequal treatment in the workplace or in the home, many of them are raising their voices in protest. These efforts on their part lead to greater self-esteem and enable them to consider themselves as worthy persons (Omvedt 1980: 136–54).

Under the influence of these various women's groups the media are beginning to play a part, though only in a small way, by offering alternate ideals and images for women to emulate instead of always promoting wifehood and motherhood. There are films, for example, that seriously confront the issues regarding the options for women and allow for solutions that promote autonomy and self reliance.[8]

Some educated young people, influenced by the new egalitarian ideals promoted by the various women's groups, are choosing their own mates and doing away with the custom of dowry. In such marriages, more often than not, the conjugal bond tends to be stronger (deSouza 1975: 37–53).

The structural separation of nuclear family due to urbanization has resulted in mothers-in-law losing direct control over their daughters-in-law (Ross 1961: 194, 152, 178–79, 282–84). This has created conditions for the development of a stronger conjugal bond and reduction of the mothers' emotional dependence on sons. It appears that the proverbial antagonism between mothers-in-law and daughters-in-law can be reduced. Without the conservative influence of the older generation, nuclear family members might become more receptive to new ideas to restructure their relationships. In some urban families, the observation of rituals related to menstruation, childbirth, and widowhood are losing popularity. Some parents are investing equally in the future of daughters as well as sons in terms of education. In some cases daughters are doing everything the sons do, including supporting the parents financially. Such personal experiences on the part of parents calls into question the publicly held beliefs regarding the intrinsic inferiority of daughters (Goldstein 1972: 97–126).

These changes are taking place mainly in a few urban areas and occasionally in rural ones. Still, these forces cannot be ignored because they indicate possibilities for the future. They also show that perhaps it is not impossible to escape from the clutches of Pativratya. Nevertheless one has to admit that the ideology of Pativratya still holds the Hindu woman's destiny in its grip.

Appendix A

CASE HISTORIES

Background information on forty-six women—twenty-three Brahmin and twenty-three Vokkaliga—was collected. The sequence of questions was not the same for all respondents, because the interviews were kept on an informal level to put the respondents at ease. The various questions were asked as the situation permitted. In the case histories the information is provided approximately in the same order as it was obtained, with only some minor modifications. The questions referred to the following areas:

1. Personal background: caste, age, education, *thavaru* size, parental family size, husband's education

2. Family structure: number of male and female children, family type, marital status, and length of stay in joint family

3. Power structure: participation in decision making, freedom of movement, financial autonomy, and frequency of visits outside the village.

4. Life-style of women: leisure-time activity, visiting pattern within the village, friendship pattern, observance of deference customs, pollution and religious rituals, work pattern, and relation to village goddess

5. Sense of self-importance: who is important in village life, whose life in the village is difficult, and whose workload is heavy

6. Level of common knowledge: awareness of family planning, laws affecting women, voting pattern

7. Aspirations for children: desire for children's education, where children should live, the quality of village life; how boys and girls should be raised

8. Focal concerns of women: family prestige, personal reputation, hard work, poverty, and children's future. These rated on a four-point scale on the basis of whether the women mention it first, second, and so on.

Information is not available for all respondents on all questions. Information on some topics like observation of deference customs is not necessarily reported for all because it is invariably observed by almost all. Nonobservance in isolated cases is pointed out. The case history includes information given verbally by the respondents. In some cases— especially among Brahmins—the actions do not reflect the verbal response. This was evident, for example, when a woman said women are as important as men but in fact did not care for herself or her daughter when sick.

THREE OF THE VOKKALIGA WOMEN WHO PARTICIPATED IN THE INTERVIEWS. NOTE THE TAPE RECORDER ON THE FLOOR AT THE LEFT.

A selected number of cases that are referred to in the text are included here. The numbers 1–23 refer to Brahmins, 24–46 to Vokkaligas.

3. *Suma* Age is 42. She married at the age of 14 and has three sons. She has eighth grade education and her husband has completed tenth. Her *thavaru* is Musali itself. Her father used to be headmaster of local secondary school and is now retired. Her parents had to take some loans for the marriage but it was not very burdensome as she is the only daughter. She has one older and one younger brother. The older brother is an engineer working in the city. The younger brother is now 27 years old and the village rumor was that intense preparations were going on for his marriage.

Suma is not happy about her marriage within the same village. She was very young when she got married and says she did not know any better. She does not have anything against her husband but growing up in the same village and living out one's entire life in this same village is, she thinks, very boring. Being the only daughter, she feels that her parents should have tried to get an educated husband for her so that she could live in a city. Her parents were very enamored of her husband's family, the richest in the village. If the rich man's property were divided, Suma says, she and her husband would probably be as poor as everyone else in the village.

She has three sons but feels sad that she does not have a daughter. It seems her husband wanted to stop after two sons but she insisted on trying for the third time in the hope of getting a daughter. She told me that she cried when the third one was a boy, too. She could not convince her husband to try again so she had to stop. Suma's husband is considered one of the pioneers in the village by being the first man to get a vasectomy done because he did not want a large family. Suma feels that a daughter decorates the house making it pleasant and lively.

Suma's daily routine is similar to other Brahmin women, except that she enjoys going to the fields and garden once in a while just to see what is growing. This is considered rather unusual for a respectable Brahmin woman to do. But Suma maintains that she would rather do this than sit at home getting bored or indulge in unnecessary gossip with someone. She does not have too much to do at home because only one of her sons is living with them now and the other two are in the city studying.

She goes to Hassan to see movies with her sons. Her husband never goes because he does not like movies. She says that she does not have many friends in the village but visits her mother and sisters-in-law (husband's brothers' wives). She has a very vague idea about the laws that affect women. She believes in family planning and is enthusiastic about advising others also. Decisions about running of the household are made by her and the money management is done jointly. She does not have to get permission from her husand to go anywhere. She usually goes to her mother for advice if she has any problems. Father-in-law is a rich man and usually helps out if they have any financial troubles. She voted for the Janata party during last elections. She thinks village life is harder only because it poses problems for childrens' education and they have to stay away from the family. She believes that the work in the village is hard on both men and women and both men and women are important in village life. About the village people, she maintains that there are both good and bad people. Suma says that she does not have many worries but is very disappointed that none of her sons is bright in studies. She wants them to become well educated and work in cities.

She admits that she has an unusual relationship with her husband and sons compared to others in the village. Her sons are known to help her out in kitchen work, washing clothes, cleaning house, in fact, much of the work only women are supposed to do. Especially on festival days, one of the sons gets up early with her and works along with her all the way. Her husband also always treats her with respect and consideration. She explains all this by saying that she has been blessed. Somehow everyone in the family loves her just as she loves them. She thinks one reason probably is that she wanted a daughter so much that her sons try to make up for it. As a person, Suma is very pleasant and friendly. She is always relaxed as she is not overworked and does not have any overwhelming problems.

4. Jaya Jaya's age is 41. *Thavaru* is Periyapatna, about 50 miles from Musali and much bigger. She has one older and one younger brother and four older sisters, all of whom are married. Father was a school-teacher. Originally they are from Agrahara, a small village, but as soon as the older brother started earning (he is an industrialist in Mysore), the father started to buy lands in Periyapatna which is a very fertile valley. The family eventually moved to Periyapatna after father's retirement. Marriage of daughters did not pose any problems to Jaya's father as all the daughters are very beautiful. The rumor is that the groom's people actually bribed the father for his daughter's hand, which was as high as Rs 500. Jaya thinks herself not as pretty as her sisters (she is modest) and besides, for the youngest daughter the parents did not take too much trouble to find a proper groom. Jaya is very unhappy that she ended up in a poor village like Musali even though her father-in-law is a rich man in the village. Moreover, she is the second wife (the first one is dead). Until she got married, Jaya lived in a city with her brother, to finish her education. She completed grade 11 education and wanted very much to pass twelfth grade, but she got married first. Her husband has twelfth grade education.

Jaya has three daughters and one son. The oldest daughter is married, and Jaya explained in detail the trouble she had to go through to perform that marriage. The biggest problem was money. They have enough to eat and drink but not much is left or saved to do anything extra. Her husband, even though he is the eldest son of a rich father, did not get much property from him. They never got along well, and the son antagonized the father further when he insisted on setting up a separate household of his own instead of living in the joint household. According to Indian laws of inheritance the sons have a right to equal share of ancestral property, but the father can divide the property accumulated through his self-effort according to his wishes. The father chose not to give Jaya's husband any part of the property he himself had accumulated which is substantial. The two older daughters of Jaya are ready for marriage, and she is very worried about their future. The loan of the first daughter's marriage is not paid off yet. Jaya is using all her ingenuity to cultivate friendship with her father-in-law but it is not working so well. Jaya is very fond of her son but is a bit disappointed because he did not become either an engineer or a doctor. He only managed to earn a B.A. and is working in some kind of clerical job in the nearby city.

Jaya's daily routine is similar to that of other Brahmin women. She sometimes has extra work as she has to cook for the hired hands. Her husband is not a very hard worker, therefore usually hires someone to do heavy work. She does not feel overworked as she has daughters to help her out. Jaya believes that life in the village is not only hard but very dull. She thinks that the work is much harder for men than women. She believes men are more important than women in village life, because, in her words, all women do is wait for men to bring things so that everyone can eat. She thinks that women have a low status because they have to depend on men for everything. It would be much better, she says, if Brahmin women were also allowed to work in the field like Vokkaliga women, then they will feel they are important. She has a kitchen garden which she takes care of by herself. She is very much concerned about improving the quality of life in the village. She played a very active role in starting a *mahila samaj* (women's society) in the village and ran it for nine years with funding from various levels of government. After nine years, the funding stopped and all that is left are the two sewing machines which are in an anteroom in her house; the billboard with title *"Mahila Samaj"* still hangs on a side of her house. Jaya blames the villagers for their pettymindedness and lack of enthusiasm, but the villagers accuse her of embezzling the money that belonged to the *samaj*, thereby putting a stop to the funding. It was very difficult to get at the "truth" of the matter.

She believes in family planning and has helped at least fifteen women in the village to get tubectomy done. She has also helped a number of villagers to get proper treatment from hospitals and doctors. She is very helpful to villagers in times of need. She is well liked by Vokkaliga women who have benefited from her intervention, but Brahmin women think of her as some kind of busybody.

Jaya is familiar with laws affecting women. She does not think that bringing up of girls is harder than boys, but it is definitely more expensive. She says that her husband makes all decisions in the family including financial and she has to obtain his permission to go anywhere. Most people in the community believe that her husband is henpecked and she is the real boss in the family. She goes to Hassan once a month to see a movie and visit her children. When asked about the nature of the village deity, she answered that she is not superstitious but goes along with everyone in the village. She believes that women also should be allowed to marry for the second time. She voted for Janata this time but used to vote for Gandhi even against her husband's wishes.

5. Shankri Her age is 32 years. She has sixth grade education and her husband has eighth. *Thavaru* is Pungami, about ten miles from Musali and about the same size. Villagers there have to depend on the monsoons just as in Musali. She got married at the age of 17 and has two sons and three daughters. One child died at a young age, and she had two miscarriages. Her marriage was an exchange marriage, but still it was difficult for the parents. They had to sell one plot of land to cover the marriage expenses. She is the only daughter of her parents. She has one older and one younger brother.

Shankri's daily routine is similar to that of other Brahmin women except that she has a 14-year-old daughter who is very helpful. Shankri thinks that it is equally hard to bring up boys and girls. She thinks that her life here is similar to that of *thavaru* as neither family is financially well off. She believes that villagers have to work very hard to get enough to eat. She brought up all the five children herself without much help from anyone. She feels overworked here as she was not used to much work in her *thavaru*. Her mother used to do all the work without relying too much on her as she was an only daughter. Shankri wants all her children to live in cities; she does not want them to suffer in a village like her.

Her husband makes all the decisions in the family, including financial. Once in a while he consults with her but may not necessarily act on her suggestions. She has to obtain his permission to go anywhere. She does not have any money of her own, therefore has to ask her husband if she needs any. If he gives, she uses it—otherwise learns to do without it. She does not go anywhere outside village except to *thavaru* and that only once in a while. She does not have many friends, as she has not time to cultivate friendship. She believes that sons and daughters have to be advised differently as they have different types of work to do in life. The daughters, especially, have to be taught much etiquette, because they have to go and live in their husband's house. She voted for the Janata, according to her husband's advice. She is not aware of any laws affecting women. She believes in family planning and is practicing it even though she started late.

She believes that city life is much better than village life because villagers are so vulnerable, depending on the vagaries of rainfall. She believes that both men and women have to work hard to make ends meet and thinks that men are more important because unless they work hard outside, the family cannot survive. With regard to the nature of the village deity Shankri thinks she is an incarnation of Parvati. She believes that worshipping the deity is important to help people develop a proper outlook towards life.

Shankri is a very hardworking woman. All the cleaning and curing of all grains and pulses is done by her. In addition, she helps her husband in his commercial activity by processing arecanut which takes a long time. She also keeps a very tidy kitchen garden which supplies daily vegetables for the family. If any more time is left over she makes leaf cups and plates (*donne, ele*) which bring in some money to subsidize weekly expenses.

Shankri's relationship with her husband is rather distant. She is terribly afraid of him as he is a quick-tempered man. His word is law in the house, and even if a little thing goes wrong like too much salt in the soup or rice gets a little overdone, he is known to fly into a rage and often beats his wife.

9. Shami Her age is 32. She has completed grade 12 education. Her husband Raju is a schoolteacher in the nearby small village. As her husband is an only son, her mother-in-law lives with them. She got married at the age of 17 and has a son and two daughters. Thavaru is Esalurpete, about 50 miles from Musali and much bigger. She has one older and three younger brothers and two younger sisters. Father is a secondary school headmaster. She thinks her marriage was not burdensome to her parents; they are relatively well-to-do and there was no dowry. The marriage was performed in a moderate fashion. Her father owns a little coffee garden also.

Shami refused to make a comparative evaluation of her life in her *thavaru* with that of Musali. Her daily routine is similar to that of other Brahmin women, except that her mother-in-law shares some of the work. Bringing up her children was not difficult as her mother-in-law was helpful. Shami does not think that there is any difference in bringing up boys and girls even though her son was more mischievous than her daughters. He also had a tendency to get sick more often. Shami wants all her children to live in the city environment. She does not believe village life is good enough for them. She visits her *thavaru* often. She is not familiar with all the laws affecting women. She goes to Hassan to see movies quite often. She voted for the Congress. She believes in family planning. About the nature of the village goddess, Sharada says she is a form of Parvati.

Her husband makes all the decisions in the family which includes financial. He might consult with her once in a while. She does not need permission to go to another house in the same village, but she does need it to go outside of the village. She has to ask for money as she has no income of her own. She can spend on anything only after obtaining permission from him and according to his wishes. If she has her own money (like a gift from her parents) she can spend it the way she likes. She believes that village life is harder for men—they have to work outside in bad weather. Men, she thinks, are more important in village life.

Shami is known as an intelligent woman among her neighbors. Her relationship with her husband tends to be more democratic than she admits. Coming from a relatively well-to-do family Shami feels that she was married beneath her. She is disappointed in her parents for not taking more trouble to marry her to someone who is equal to their status. Raju is an intelligent man and a very understanding husband. He often feels very unhappy because he cannot provide all the comforts his wife is used to.

Shami is a very hardworking woman. In addition to housework she has a very nicely kept kitchen garden of which she is very proud. She says they never have a meal without vegetables, thanks to her garden. She also sews all of her clothes and her daughters'. If she has time she sews clothes for other villagers also which earns her some pocket money. She invariably spends it on clothing for her children because she wants them as well dressed as her brother's children in the city.

10. Sharada Her age is 30. She has an eighth grade education, and so does her husband. *Thavaru* is Uttanuru, about 200 miles from Musali and much bigger. It is a big village with all the conveniences. She got married at the age of 21 and has two sons (two daughters died at the age of two). Her marriage was not very difficult as no dowry was involved. She has one older and one younger brother and one younger sister. While her children were small she had her mother-in-law living with her, therefore she did not have much problem. Sharada's daily routine is similar to that of other Brahmin women. She does not feel that she is overworked as there are no small children in the house and as she does not have to do any work outside the home.

Sharada does not think that there is any difference in bringing up boys and girls. She believes that life in this village and life in her *thavaru* are similar. She does not often go out of the village except to visit her mother once a year and to Hassan just to see movies about once every three months. She cannot say whether city life is much better than village life since she has not lived in a city. She thinks that village life is harder for men. As for her children, she does not mind their staying either in the village or town as long as they are educated and have good jobs. Because of the unpredictability of monsoons she thinks that people in the village are vulnerable. She is not aware of any laws affecting women. She believes in family planning because she thinks people should have as many children as they can take care of. She cannot say anything about the nature of the village goddess.

Most decisions in the house are made jointly. Money management is in husband's hands, but he might consult her now and then. She does not have to get permission to go to other people's houses in the same village. Whenever they go out of the village, they do it usually together. She cannot say whether women or men are more important in village life. She thinks that children should be guided properly to develop good conduct. She says that people in the village are good if oneself is good.

Sharada's relationship with her husband is amicable. They are known to the neighbors as quiet people minding their own business. Suri, Sharada's husband, is not a very hardworking man. He would rather live within his means than work too hard to make extra money. He does his usual daily routine of worshiping the temple deity and keeping the inner courtyard clean, as it is his job, and sits around the rest of the time. Sharada thinks that he can earn extra money if he works harder on the little plot of land they own. Sharada, on the other hand, does not mind working hard if that means having more money but she does not know what to do. She complains that there are no opportunities in the village to make extra money even if one wants to. Though she does not approve of Suri's behavior, she does not make an issue out of it. She is concentrating on the children and helping them to do well in school.

11. Gowri Her age is 39. She has a fourth grade education and can read and write Kannada. Her husband has eight years of schooling. Her *thavaru* is Marthamnalli, which is smaller than Musali and which also depends on the monsoons. She got married at the age of 18 and has two sons and one daughter. She has three older sisters, one younger and three older brothers. All brothers and sisters are married. As all marriages were exchange marriages, no dowry was involved. The marriages were not celebrated with much pomp or ceremony.

Gowri's daily routine is similar to that of other Brahmin women except that she sometimes helps out in light garden work like picking fruits or weeding. Her 17-year-old daughter helps with daily household chores, so she does not feel overworked. When the children were small she had her elder brother's daughter living with her to help out. Therefore she has never felt overworked.

Gowri does not feel that village life is all that hard but wants all her children to live in cities. It is because she thinks that the quality of village life is bad; people are jealous and quarrelsome. The villagers cannot stand anyone getting ahead. Gowri and her husband are both shrewd and hardworking. Among relatively poor people some ten years ago, right now they are thought of as being relatively well-to-do. Gowri thinks this has made all the villagers envious of them. Both of her sons have graduated from college and are looking for jobs in Bangalore. She wants to marry her daughter to a well-educated man with a good job. She says that she does not have any friends in the village, therefore does not visit anyone often. Decisions about daily life are made jointly, and the same is true of financial management. She voted for the Janata during the elections. She is not aware of any laws affecting women. She says that she is not interested in family planning but neighbors say that her husband had a vasectomy several years ago. Gowri thinks that to make children follow the right path parents should give proper advice and see to it that they move around in good company. She believes that boys should be advised differently from girls.

Gowri is known in the community as a domineering woman. Her husband is considered as being completely under her control. Most people in the community are afraid to talk to her as she is believed to have a sharp tongue. Her only daughter also is believed to be turning out just like her. It is believed that all the efforts they are putting to arrange the daughter's marriage are not successful precisely because of the bad reputation Gowri has developed in the village.

12. *Lalli* Her age is 47. Her *thavaru* is Pungame, which is smaller than Musali. Its water resource is a tank, just as in Musali. She has four brothers and four sisters. She has an eigthth grade education, and so does her husband. She got married at the age of 13 and has five sons and two daughters. Her marriage was not very difficult as no dowry was given.

One of her sons and one of her daughters are married. One son is working in a nearby town as a clerk in an office. Her eldest son takes care of the land. Third son is helping her husband operate a flour mill and a rice mill which they started about six years ago. The other sons (age 12 and 10) are going to school. One daughter (age 18) is still living with her, and the elder daughter is in her husband's house. Lalli's family is believed to be well-to-do in the village. She lives in a joint family along with her son and his wife.

Lalli believes that village life is harder than that of city life—much harder for women. She wants all her children to live in cities. She has

some friends in the village. She visits Hassan and Bangalore to see relatives and sometimes catches a movie or two. As her close relatives live
in Hassan she does not have to worry about where to stay. Besides, one
of her sons has a room in Hassan since he is studying there. She is
ambivalent about the quality of life in the village. She voted for the Janata
Party; knows about laws affecting women. She believes in family planning
but was not aware of it until recently.

She makes most of the decisions in the family, including financial.
She says it is because her husband does not want to be bothered with
them and also she is much more competent. She does not have to get
anyone's permission to go anywhere or do anything. Even to spend
money, she says, she does not have to ask anyone. She believes that
children should be given proper advice to turn out well. She thinks that
girls and boys should be brought up differently. She believes that both
men and women are important in village life. With regard to the village
deity, Lalli believes she is an auspicious goddess. If you show devotion
to her anything gets done.

Lalli is considered as a very smart woman by most villagers. It is
generally believed that it is only her initiative that led to the starting of
the flour mill and rice mill which are making very good profit. Recently
they began building a house in Hassan, as Lalli believes that it will be
good to have property in urban area. She is believed to be a very good
business woman capable of managing the money.

Lalli's relationship with her husband is considered odd by most
villagers. She is believed to be bossy and her husband, Kittu, is henpecked.
Most people make fun of him behind his back. No one dare say anything
in front of him as he is a very short-tempered man and such an event
has led to serious fistfights in the past. It appears that Kittu is not a
hardworking man but likes to be rich. He does not see anything wrong
in taking his wife's advice. Even though people believe Lalli makes all
decisions (Lalli confided in me that she in fact does make all decisions),
Kittu protests very strongly and maintains that she only gives advice. In
fact all property is either in his name or in his eldest son's name. Lalli
behaves as though she could not care less about the criticisms people
make about her relationship with her husband and her role in the family.
The most important thing, as far as she is concerned, is that her children
should be well settled and her family become prosperous. On an interpersonal level Lalli and her husband have an amicable relationship. Lalli
does not follow all the deference customs rigorously.

15. Vanajamma Her age is 53 years. *Thavaru* is Hassan, about eight
miles from Musali. She got married at the age of 12 and has five sons
and one daughter. One daughter committed suicide, and one son died
of pneumonia. Parents have died. Father used to be a clerk in a govern-

ment office. She has two older and two younger brothers and one younger sister. Her marriage was not hard on her father because there was no dowry involved. All her brothers are educated. She has completed eight years of education. Her husband has twelve years of education. Her daily routine is similar to that of other Brahmin women. She has a daughter-in-law who helps her with the housework. One daughter-in-law got separated from the joint family and is living in a different house. The second daughter-in-law is with her and is obedient to her.

She frequently visits her relatives in Mysore and Hassan. The decisions regarding expenditure of money are handled by her. She does not have to ask her husband's permission to visit anyone or go anywhere. It is common knowledge in the community that Vanajamma and her husband are not on good terms. Even though a formal distance is maintained and deference is shown to him, basic hostility between them surfaces too often. It is difficult to say who is at fault even though everyone tends to blame her unwomanly behavior—talking loud, arguing. Her complaint is often about his not caring for her and her feelings. Ramappa dismisses the whole thing, saying that it is his bad deeds in his past life that made him end up with this wife. She believes that women are more important in life because they are responsible for making ends meet and keep things rolling smoothly.

She did not vote this time. She would have voted for the Janata as everyone she knew did so. She does not know about any laws affecting women nor about family planning. In fact, she prefers big families. She believes in worshipping the village deity because she thinks that she is good to those who are faithful. She grew up in a city but ended up in a village, and she is not happy about it. She thinks that village life is hard for both men and women. She believes that children can be made into upright citizens if parents give them proper advice. They should be told to avoid bad company. She does not think that there is any difference in the way daughters and sons are brought up.

She is very happy with the way her children have turned out. Several of them have studied well, and some are helping with farming. Her daughter is living in town. One of her sons is in a town also. Husband is very lazy. Tends to wander off to various villages and nearby cities and comes home whenever he pleases. The sons are hardworking, and she is very proud of them.

She does not get along with any of the daughters-in-law. She is especially bitter about her first one because the son set up his own family separately. Even though they live in different houses there are frequent quarrels, each abusing the other. Vanajamma always sounds louder if she feels that she is not getting any sympathy from anyone, especially her husband and sons. She threatens suicide and has attempted it five or six times. She also suffers from spirit possession; whenever that happens the daughter-in-law is abused even more. The second daughter-in-law is still very docile. The second son is with the mother all the way. He has gone even to the extent of beating his wife severely when his mother complained of misbehavior on her part.

16. Seema Her age is 27. Her *thavaru* is Lingadanahalli, which is bigger than Musali and has many shops and a bus station. She got married at the age of 23 and has a daughter. She has ten years of schooling. Her husband has twelve years of schooling. She had a younger sister but she died at the age of 4. Father is a landlord. She does not visit her *thavaru* often. She did not even go there for her confinement during her first pregnancy, even though it is always customary. Her daughter is 2 years old now. It seems the marriage was performed by her uncle in Mandya. No dowry was paid. The uncle bore all the expenses of marriage. I tried to probe and get the information as to why her parents did not do it. Except for saying that she was never close to her parents she refused to say anything more about them. She lives in joint family along with her parents-in-law. Her daily routine is similar to women of her caste. She does not feel overworked.

All decisions in the house are made by the mother-in-law. She is not consulted at any time. Her husband takes care of money management and consults his mother often. If she has to go anywhere in the village, she needs the permission of her mother-in-law. If she has to go out of town, then she needs the permission of both her mother-in-law and her husband. She voted for the Janata as everyone in the family did. She is not aware of any laws affecting women. She believes in family planning but does not want to get the operation done because she is afraid that it might make her physically weak. But she does not want more than two children. She wants her children to study and work in a city, but she thinks that village life is better than city life. When I asked her to explain this contradiction, she said that village life is good enough for her but not for her children. She believes that village life is harder for men because men have to work outdoors whereas women work only indoors. She thinks that both men and women are necessary to make a go of it in the village. She believes that her life here is better than in *thavaru* as everyone is nice to her. She had nothing to say about the village deity. She does not have any close friends.

The neighbor's evaluation of her situation is completely different. All of them think that she is completely dominated by her mother-in-law, who has the reputation of being a very strong-willed woman used to having her own way. My observation of her behavior in front of her mother-in-law confirmed the neighbor's assessment.

Her relationship with her husband is very formal. They are never seen together. She follows all the deference customs scrupulously. She works very hard from morning till night, eats whatever is given to her after everyone has eaten. One never hears her complain about anything. She generally looks very sad and withdrawn. She is very devoted to God and sings many devotional songs beautifully.

17. Venki Age 66. *Thavaru* is Pungame. Illiterate. Married at age of 15. She was an only child of her parents. Her marriage was not hard on anyone as no dowry was involved, and it was a simple marriage. She lost her parents when she was only about a year old in a plague epidemic. Her cousin (mother's older sister's daughter) brought her up. Her father had quite a bit of property but his brothers took it and did not give her anything. As she was a child and did not have any well-wishers who would fight for her rights she lost everything when she lost her parents. Her cousin was very affectionate towards her. Her husband died when she was only 25, leaving five children, three daughters and two sons, in her care.

Being a young widow with five small children, without help from anyone, she had to work outdoors most of the time associating with men of other castes. This was considered unbecoming for a Brahmin woman who should lead a retired life praying to God and atoning for her past sins. She had her head shaven and was wearing only red *sarees* as widows should. But she refused to stay home and continued with her business of buying and selling as she thought that it was the only way she could provide for her children. She could not do farmwork because she did not have the physical strength. Her behavior brought the wrath of the Brahmin community on her. Rumors were circulated that she was having illicit sexual relations with men of other castes. Even though no one had any proof of this, everyone believed it anyway. She was ostracized by the Brahmin community, but she still did not budge from her stance and went about her life the same way. Then yet another rumor was circulated that she poisoned people. In fact it was believed that she had the magical power to destroy anyone as she is a witch. Even to this day most people in the village are afraid even to take water from her. I was strongly advised not to go near her house and not to touch any food she might offer me. Her children suffered also as no one would play with them or invite them to their houses. When time for marriage came no one would marry her daughters or give any daughters to her sons. Finally her eldest daughter married an old man as second wife. A daughter Radha was born to them but soon after the old man died. Radha was married to Venki's second son. Venki's eldest son had to marry an ugly destitute girl—a Brahmin. The other two daughters married out-of-state Brahmins who had no contact or knowledge of Venki's life. From what I hear, they are happy and have two children each.

Venki says she has no regrets as she did the best she could under the circumstances. She claims that all the allegations about her personal life were false and intended just to hurt her pride. She feels sorry about the hardship brought to her children, but she could see no alternative. She is bitter about the way everyone treated her but says she does not want to remember those days anymore. She says that only God is her witness, and she has taken care of her children well.

Her relationship with her daughter-in-law is very bad. She is known as one of the most cruel mothers-in-law that ever lived. The daughter-in-law has been beaten, burnt, starved, and abused. The son has been her accomplice in everything. She has several grandchildren whom she loves dearly.

Her daily routine is similar to many Brahmin women except that she works much harder. She has her daughter-in-law do most of the household chores, and she takes care of outside chores. She manages her farm, recruits hired hands, takes care of cattle, buys and sells things.

She is a very energetic, competent woman and leads a very busy life. Even though she is close to 66 she looks barely in her early 50s. Even when she is home taking some rest she works with her hands, making some leaf cups or leaf plates.

She thinks that bringing up boys and girls is not very significantly different. As she has no experience of living in a city she cannot say anything about comparing that way of life with this. She has always lived in a village and has learned to cope with it. Actually, she believes that life in the city may be harder because people have to buy everything, whereas in the village one can grow so many things one uses and one does not have to pay rent. She goes to *sante* (village fair) regularly as it is her business to sell and buy things. She has friends in nearby villages and in Musali also as it is required to make a success of her business ventures. The farmers in the village, she says, have always been very helpful to her in many ways in times of trouble. But, the Brahmins were of no help to her anytime in her life.

She voted for the Janata Party. She is not aware of any laws affecting women. She believes in a small family but does not want anyone sterilized. Now that she is old, she is not going to worry about anything. She believes that village life is hard for everyone as making a living means working hard. When her husband was alive all the decisions in the household including financial were made by him. But after his death she was left alone, the responsibility fell on her, and she has been making them since then. Nowadays she consults her son before deciding on anything. She thinks it is good to worship the village deity every year as she is of good nature. She thinks that men are more important in village life. To make children good people they should be given education and good advice. Besides, if the parents are good, children usually turn out good.

18. *Shanta* Her age is 53. She has three years of schooling and her husband has eight. She was born and brought up in a city where her father had a salaried job. She got married at the age of 11 and she has four daughters and three sons. She has one elder brother, and two younger sisters. She lost both parents at the age of 12. Her marriage was not very expensive since her sister's marriage also was performed at the same time without any dowry in both cases. Her father did not have to take any loans, as he had saved enough for the marriage. The father's insurance money paid for both her youngest sister's marriage and her brother's education. After the parents died, her mother's brother and his wife took care of them. She has very unhappy memories of those days since she was treated very badly. The money, jewelry, household utensils—all those things that were left by her parents were appropriated by them. She is very bitter about losing both parents immediately after marriage and having to live in her uncle's family for a few years before she was old enough to move to her husband's house. She was very close to her father and loved him dearly. Her memory is still fresh about each little thing he said and did. She does not have pleasant memories about her mother as she was terribly afraid of her. Shanta is very disappointed in her parents for marrying her into a village like this. She thinks that it is the worst thing anyone could do to a daughter.

The man she is married to is a very hardworking farmer. He lost his father when he was a baby and his mother when he was about 8. He is the youngest in the family, with one older brother and one older sister. He was virtually brought up by his aunt and sister-in-law, as they all lived in a joint family. He did not get much love and affection from anyone. Shanta's relationship with her husband is rather cold. They never talk to each other and go about doing their own daily chores. Shanta scrupulously follows all deference customs including eating in the same plate her husband has eaten from after he has finished his meal.

Her relationship with her children is very cold also except with her first son. She has a worried look on her face almost all the time. She sits and broods a lot in her spare time. She was not involved in family decision making when they were living with her in-laws as the family was run by them. But even after they got separated and started living on their own, she shows no interest in family life.

Her daily routine is similar to that of other Brahmin women except that she has the help of grown daughters which gives her some spare time to do the things she likes most, namely prayer and worship. While the children were young, work was physically strenuous; now it is not so. She does not think that there is any difference in hardship between bringing up boys and girls. Both are the same as neither of them have given her any trouble. Life in the husband's house she considers better than living with her uncle. It is because that is where a woman is supposed to be. She thinks that life in a city is much easier and more civilized than life in the village, therefore she wants all her children to live in a city. She does not go out of the village except to visit her daughter and son who are living in cities.

Decisions, including financial, are made by the husband; she is not consulted on anything. She does not have to ask for permission to visit anyone. She has no money of her own, and she can go out of town only when her husband sends her. She voted for the Janata as everyone in the family did. She is not aware of any laws affecting women. She believes very strongly in family planning and wants her children to follow it. She herself wanted to follow it but her husband, who does not believe in it, refused. She believes that men are more important in village life as it is they who work hard outside and bring things home. Women only take care of household things which is not all that important. She strongly believes that parents should advise their children properly so that they do not go into bad ways. The village goddess she thinks is not of bad temperament but a good one, and she satisfies the desires of her devotees.

Of her six children, two sons have become engineers and gotten good jobs. Her eldest daughter has married an engineer. The second daughter is about to be married to a rich man who has studied for a B. Com. Her second son also is going to be married soon. The third and last daughters are studying at Bangalore. The youngest son has stayed in the village to take care of the lands. By village standards Shanta can be considered a most fortunate woman as her sons are educated and daughters are getting married. No matter how much anyone reminds her of her good fortune, Shanta is a very unhappy woman.

19. Latha Her age is about 39. Her *thavaru* is Pungame which is smaller than Musali. She married at the age of 17 and has two sons and one daughter. She has completed 7 years of education, and her husband has 14. She has 6 brothers and 3 sisters. Father is not alive, and the brothers are managing the family. Her marriage was not very difficult; the dowry was not very big, and her father was still alive. Besides, one of her brothers is working in the military and making good money. She expects that the marriage of her other sisters is going to be difficult as the brothers will soon have their own families and the dowry has gone up in recent years.

Latha's daily routine is similar to that of other Brahmins. She does not think that her daily life is very strenuous for her; her daughter is 20 years old and is very helpful. Of the two sons, the younger is studying in Bangalore and the older is staying in the village at this time because he failed an exam. He is hoping to pass the second time. While the children were small, Latha's mother-in-law lived with them and was very helpful.

Latha believes that village life is much harder than life in the city. She does not think that her life was any better in her *thavaru* as there also people had to depend on the unpredictable monsoons to make a living. She believes that her own life is worse than that of her mother and hopes that her children's lives will be better. Village life, she thinks, is much harder for men. In daily life she believes that both men and women are needed since both have to work to make a go of it. She visits her *thavaru* and Hassan once in awhile. She has not seen any movies so far. Decisions in the house are made jointly. With regard to financial matters, her husband is in control, but he does consult her often. She does not have to ask for permision to go anywhere in the village but to go outside of the village she needs permission. She has to ask for money if she needs any, but she can spend the money she got in the form of presents from her brothers or other relatives whatever way she likes. She voted for the Janata. She has heard of laws affecting women but does not know the details. She believes in family planning. She believes that to make children turn out good, parents should give proper advice and that is all they can do. Latha believes that it is easier to convince girls, but boys tend to be more stubborn. Even though she knows that people worship the village deity, she does not know why, nor does she know what her nature is.

Latha broods a lot because she has many worries. Her husband is a weak man, both in terms of physical strength and strength of will. He never worked hard enough on the 2½ acres of land they own to make a good living even in times of good weather. Unfortunately, the weather has been very bad for the last two years which has destroyed their arecanut plants. These need a lot of care and attention and take at least six years to start bearing fruit. Vasu, Latha's husband, worked as hard as he could on about 50 seedlings for two years. The plants were doing fine and in four years they would have given a very big crop which would have eased their burden. But the bad weather destroyed all the seedlings, and Vasu has become heartbroken. He has become very weak, and people say that he has lost the will to live. In addition to this problem, Latha worries because her sons are not doing well in school and her daughter is not married.

Latha's relationship with her husband is considered to be good by her neighbors. She is a soft-spoken woman with solicitous mannerisms. But Vasu is thought a misfit in the village; he lacks manly aggressiveness and tends to give up easily.

27. *Sathamma* Age 55 years. She is illiterate. *Thavaru* is Grama, about nine miles from Musali and much bigger. It has all the conveniences of a small town. As the canal is close by there is no problem about water supply. Father was a rich man and uncle is the chairman of the Panchayat committee in the village. Sathamma is very proud of her prestigious family. Even though brideprice was in vogue when she got married, her father refused it. She was married at the age of 18.

Sathamma has two children, a son and a daughter, both of whom are married. Her husband is a retired schoolteacher. They both live with their married son who has three sons and one daughter. Sathamma's daughter is married to a rich man who lives in a small town.

Sathamma does not do much work around the house as it is her daughter-in-law's job. She mainly takes care of outside affairs like managing the hired hands, buying and selling produce, and taking care of the cattle. Their family is considered as one of the better-off families in the village. They have a servant girl who helps around the house and two regular hired hands to help with the outside work. Sathamma's husband has become rather weak because he is old and therefore does not do much work. Besides, since he always engaged in teaching while he was young, he had left all the farm management in the hands of his wife. The same tradition has continued. Sathamma's son also is a schoolteacher and does not take much interest in farm work. The consequence is that Sathamma is left with the bulk of the responsibilites.

Sathamma is very competent in her work. She goes to the fair every week and visits the nearby town often. She also visits her *thavaru* and her daughter often. Decisions at home are made jointly. Monetary affairs are mainly taken care of by the husband, but Sathamma is consulted often. She does not have to ask for permission to go outside the house but she has to if she wants to go outside the village. Even though she does not keep the money in her own hands, she says that she has no problem getting it whenever she needs any. She voted for the Janata Party as all the family members did. She says that she knows all the laws concerning women but some probing revealed that she is not very knowledgeable. She believes in family planning and was instrumental in making her daughter-in-law get a tubectomy. She thinks that boys and girls should be brought up differently. She believes that village life is harder than city life for both men and women. She believes that both men and women are important in village life.

Sathamma tends to brag quite a bit while answering. She does not think much of people in Musali, and they do not measure up to the people in her *thavaru*, according to her asessment. She is not very happy about the kind of husband her parents got for her. In her opinion she could have gotten a better person considering the prestige of her *thavaru*. Her relationship with her husband is formal, and neighbors think that she does not respect him much and tends to be bossy.

She does not get along with her daughter-in-law, Saroja. The village gossip is that Sathamma has been instrumental in alienating her son and daughter-in-law. She is very close to her son who always took his mother's side every time there was a quarrel between the two women. Very often the incident was carried too far, and the wife was beaten. The tension in the family became too great and the son took up drinking and made a regular habit of beating his wife. Finally Sathamma's husband had to interfere and bring about a temporary truce. The beatings have stopped, and the son's drinking also has reduced a great deal. But Sathamma is not on speaking terms with her daughter-in-law.

29. *Lakshmi* Her age is 18 years, she has eight years of schooling. Lakshmi, affectionately nicknamed as "Jani" (meaning a smart girl), is married to a rich man's son in the same village. She has been married only two years and has a daughter six months old. She has three younger and three older brothers and one older sister. The sister is married into the same village also. Her father is considered as one of the rich men in the village and exercises considerable influence on village politics. Jani is very proud of her *thavaru* and claims that her husband's family is not as rich. But she is not unhappy about the match because her husband is studying at college in a nearby town. Her dream is for her husband to get a job in a city so that she can live there.

Jani stays home with her small child and works only inside the house. She lives in a joint family along with her parents-in-law, two brothers-in-law, and one unmarried sister-in-law. Her mother-in-law leaves all the housework in Jani's hands and pays attention to work outside the house. Jani's sister-in-law is supposed to help her inside the house but this always is not the case. Jani grumbles a lot because she finds it very difficult to take care of the little baby and do all the housework. She thinks that village life is much harder than life in the city. She believes that it is much harder for the men who are always expected to work in the fields in all kinds of weather and provide for the family. Jani thinks that women help the men and get to stay home if they have little children. All the decisions in the house are made by her parents-in-law which includes financial. Jani does not have any money of her own and has to ask for it whenever she needs any. She has to ask permission to go out of the village; to visit people in the village she does not always have to, but she should let everyone know where she is going and why. She believes that men are more important in village life. She has heard of laws affecting women but does not know the details.

She voted for Congress because she did not want to vote for Janata. When I asked her why, she did not know the exact reason. She wants all her children to study and live in cities. She believes that bringing up daughters is difficult because they are expensive. She believes in family planning and intends to follow it herself. When I asked her about the village deity, her answer was that the deity lets the worshipper know if she is pleased and one's wish will come true if the flower on the right side slides down.

Jani is known in the village as being very proud and haughty. The rumor is that because her father is a very powerful man in the village, her in-laws are unable to exercise any control over her. She is the youngest child of her parents and everyone thinks she has been spoiled because she always got whatever she wanted. Jani follows all the deference customs and thinks that she is as good as a Brahmin woman, which is unusual among Vokkaliga women in this village.

35. Thayamma Age is about 50. *Thavaru* is Halli, about six miles from Musali and slightly smaller in size. She got married at the age of 18 and has two daughters and four sons. Both her daughters and one son are married. The married son is living in the same family. She is illiterate and her husband has four years of schooling.

Her daily routine is similar to that of other women in her caste except that she has a daughter-in-law to help out. Now that all her children are older she mainly works outside in the fields. She tends the buffalo herself and sells the milk to the dairy. Milk money is her own to spend the way she likes. She visits the weekly *sante* to sell bananas and buy whatever is needed for the house. She goes to Hassan frequently as she has relatives to visit and also to see the movies.

All decisions including financial are made by the husband. He consults her often. She has to obtain permission if she has to go out of town but not if she is visiting someone within the village. As she has the milk money she does not have to ask him if she needs any money. She thinks that both men and women are important in village life. She does not approve of women marrying for the second time. She believes that it is customary for women to stay in their husband's house and take care of the children if the husband dies. She thinks that boys and girls should be given different kinds of advice to grow up properly. She believes in family planning and intends to advise her children to follow it. As for herself she feels that it is too late as she is already old. She thinks village life is harder than city life and is worse for women. She is not aware of any laws affecting women. She voted for the Janata as everyone in the family did. About the village goddess she says that she has a good temperament.

Thayamma is a pleasant person—very easy to talk to. She answers questions easily and clearly. She feels that her life is happy now, but she has many memories of difficulties she went through during the early years of marriage. That was the time when her husband was having an extramarital affair. This was a big blow to her prestige; most villagers blamed her and laughed at her for not being able to control her husband.

In addition she had to cope with her mother-in-law and do all the work at home even when she had a small baby. At the present time, the husband has mellowed and is considerate towards her. She has an amicable relationship with her daughter-in-law.

37. Jayamma She is not sure of her age but looks about 50. *Thavaru* is Ambogodanahalli. She got married at the age of 18, to her mother's brother. She did not bear any children, therefore husband married for the second time to her parallel cousin. She is illiterate and so is her husband.

Jayamma's daily routine is similar to that of other Vokkaliga women, except that she works mostly outside the house, as she does not have any small children to take care of. She goes to *sante* every week to sell and buy things. She does not have much time to cultivate friendship as she has lots of work to do all the time. Goes to Hassan once in a while to visit relatives and maybe to see a movie.

Husband takes care of all the decision making in the family, including financial. Sometimes he asks her for suggestions. She has to ask his permission if she has to go out of the village and if she needs money. She did not vote this year. If she did, she says, she would have voted for the same party the others in the family has voted for. She is not aware of any laws affecting women. She does not have any opinion about family planning, and she believes that it is up to the persons concerned. She says that village life is comfortable for her but cannot say anything about which life is better. She refused to express an opinion about whether village life is comfortable for both men and women.

Jayamma feels overwoked all the time. She says it is very difficult working in all kinds of weather outside the house. She feels a void in her life as she did not bear any children. That pain was very intense most of her life but now she has become reconciled to that. Even though she did not like the idea of her husband having another wife, she had no choice but to agree to it. She feels that her life was much happier in her *thavaru* as she did not have anything to worry about.

38. Puttamma Age is 40. Her *thavaru* is Bastihalli, which is about 1 mile from Musali and the same size. She got married at the age of 14 without any dowry as it was not common at the time. She is illiterate. She has two sons and one daughter but lost her husband about ten years ago. She had a great deal of difficulty bringing up children all by herself. This problem was made worse as one of the daughters has a club foot.

Puttamma's daily life is similar to many other Vokkaliga women's. She has to take care of work both inside the house and in the field. She feels that her life was much better in her *thavaru*. She believes that village life is hard for everyone. Therefore she wants her children to settle down in cities. She does not go out of the village often except to visit the weekly *sante* to buy the needed things. She does not have many friends because she has no time to cultivate friendship. As she does not have much land, she has to supplement the farm income through daily labor.

She is not aware of any laws affecting women. She is ambivalent about family planning. She thinks that people in the village are okay. She does not think women should marry a second time. She believes that men are more important even though she does not know the reason for it. As women have to work both inside and outside, she believes that life is relatively much harder for women.

While her husband was alive he used to make all decisions in the house, including financial. She had to ask permission to go out and ask for money if she needed it. Now she has to do everything herself. Since his death she feels that she has been burdened with all kinds of responsibilities. She wants her children to become well educated no matter how difficult it is for her.

Puttamma is distraught with life. She yearns for the old days when there was peace and security in her *thavaru*. She suffers from terrible poverty and believes that being born a woman is the worst thing that can happen to a person.

39. Basamma Her age is 21 years. She is illiterate and so is her husband. Her *thavaru* is Patna which is about 9 miles from Musali and smaller in size. People have to depend on the village reservoir for their water supply. She has five brothers and two sisters. She got married at the age of 18 and has one son. Her mother-in-law lives with the family.

Her daily routine is similar to that of other women in her caste. She has to work both inside and outside the house. She thinks that village life is harder than city life and wants her children to become educated and settle down in a city. She thinks that people in her *thavaru* are friendlier than here. She does not have many friends since she is still rather new to the village. She believes that worshipping the village deity is good for her family's welfare.

Decisions in the house are made jointly, including financial ones. She does not need permission to go to other people's houses in the village, only if she is going out of the village. She has to ask for money if she needs any as she does not have an independent income. She is not familiar with any laws affecting women, and she believes in family planning. She did not vote this year. Even though some women marry for the second time, she does not approve of it. She believes that both men and women are important in village life.

Basamma is a young person. Being very new to the village, she feels like an outsider. Mother-in-law and daughter-in-law do not get along.

She is pregnant for the second time. Even though the mother-in-law is not very old, she does not come to do any work around the house which makes Basamma's life more difficult. The village gossip is that Basamma has effectively isolated her mother-in-law and her husband is under her control. Within a short time after marriage she has managed to achieve this mainly because her husband does not have a good relationship with his mother.

40. Rangamma Age is 19 years. She is illiterate, and her husband has four years of education. She got married only a few months ago. Her *thavaru* is Kanchena Halli which is about 8 miles from Musali and smaller. Her parents had to give Rs 1000 dowry and take care of all the expenses. She feels sad that her parents did not give her any jewelry. She has one older and three younger brothers and one younger sister.

Being a young bride in a new place Rangamma feels very lonely and lost. Her mother-in-law is known among the neighbors as a taskmaster. As soon as the daughter-in-law came she stopped doing any work. The sickness (which is considered very mild by neighbors) of her husband is used as an excuse for her whiling the time away. Rangamma has a 14-year-old sister-in-law but she is of no help either, because she is going to school, and also the mother-in-law says that work is cut out for her daughter in her own in-law's house, therefore, she should relax here. Rangamma has to work both inside and in the fields. She says except for a few hours of sleep she does not get any rest.

Rangamma is not involved in any kind of decision making in the family as she is treated as an outsider. All the decisions are made by the in-laws. She has to take permission even to go and visit the neighbors. She has no money of her own, therefore she has to ask for it if she needs any but very rarely she gets any. She did not vote; no one asked her. She is not aware of any laws affecting women. She has no opinion about family planning. With regard to the village deity also she had nothing to say. She feels very uncomfortable in this village and thinks that people of Musali are very loud. She feels sorry for herself because she has to do so much work and wishes that she also had gone to school like her sister-in-law.

She wants her children to become well educated. She believes that village life is harder than city life. Therefore she wants her children to settle down in the city. She believes that village life is hard for both men and women and thinks that women are more important in village life because they work harder both inside and in the fields.

Rangamma had difficulty in answering some of the questions. Often she was afraid to express an opinion. This was especially so if questions were about relationships between family members. She was afraid that the neighbors might tell on her to her mother-in-law.

43. *Kittamma* Age is about 40 years. She is illiterate, and so is her husband. Her *thavaru* is Marenahalli which is about 2 miles form Musali and bigger. People depend on the village reservoir for water supply but there is tap water for drinking. She got married at the age of 22. Her father had two sons and three daughters. Kittamma lost her mother when she was three months old and was brought up by her stepmother. She lived a very difficult life with her in-laws for fifteen years. She does not want to remember the hardships she had to go through. Kittamma herself has six sons and four daughters. She is sending all her sons and one of her daughters to school. One son lives in a nearby town with his wife. She brought up all her children by herself without any help from anyone. She said that it was very difficult.

Kittamma's daily routine is similar to other women of her caste. She works very hard both inside and outside and feels overworked. She wants her sons to live in the city, and she feels that city life is more comfortable. All her daughters are married into villages since none of them except the youngest has any education. She visits the weekly fair once in a while when she has the urge to see a movie. One of her daughters is pregnant and therefore she goes to visit her quite often. She does not have too many friends as she has no time to cultivate friendship.

All decisions including financial are mostly made by the husband. He may consult her on matters other than financial often and sometimes on financial matters also. She has to ask permission to be outside the village. She has no independent income and therefore has to ask her husband whenever she needs any money. She voted for the Congress, as her husband asked her to. She is not aware of any laws affecting women. She has a radio in the house and listens to it once in a while. She believes that family planning is going too far, and two children are too few and risky. She is going to advise her children to have at least two sons before they decide to adopt the family planning technique. She believes that village life is hard on both men and women and both are important in village life. About the village goddess, she said that she is also called Dyavamma. She believes that the people are the same in her *thavaru* and Musali. Her life also, she thinks, is not much different.

Neighbors think Kittamma is a very intelligent wife. Even though her husband has a great deal of respect in her judgment and consults her often, she makes it a point to give the impression to others that he makes all the decisions. She takes care of her family well, and it has prospered because of her many ideas, one of which is raising several buffaloes and selling milk.

45. *Manjamma* Manjamma's age is about 28. She is illiterate, and so is her husband. She got married at the age of 18 and has two sons and one daughter. Her *thavaru* is Hallalli, about 5 miles from Musali and much smaller. She has one brother and four sisters. Manjamma says that it was very difficult for her father to marry all four daughters. None of her children is going to school. Manjamma feels that as they are very poor it is no use going to school. She cannot afford it anyway. They own a very small plot of land, and unless she works for daily wages they cannot make ends meet. Her husband is very lazy and gets drunk often. Manjamma somehow has to run the family with the help of her children, one of whom is 10 years old.

Manjamma's daily routine is similar to women in the caste except it is harder. She has to work inside and out and manage the household herself as the husband refuses to help. She does not go anywhere outside the village. She does not have any friends. She does not think anyone in the village would help her if she were in trouble. She believes that similar advice is given to boys and girls depending on what is appropriate. She voted during elections but does not know for whom. She is not aware of any laws affecting women. She believes in family planning and intends to get an operation done, but her husband is against it. She is afraid to go against her husband's wishes. Manjamma does not believe that a woman should marry for the second time especially if she has children. About the village deity she says that her name is Dyavamma.

Manjamma is very bitter because she has to make all decisions herself including financial without any help from anyone. Her husband is slightly mentally retarded, according to neighbors, as he behaves irrationally and impetuously. He is seen beating the children and wife with the slightest provocation. At other times he just sits there even when the children are misbehaving. Manjamma is a very unhappy woman. She burst into tears several times when she talked about her desperate poverty and the abuse of her husband.

46. Dyavamma Dyavamma's age is about 40. She is illiterate, and so is her husband. Her *thavaru* is Pura, about 2½ miles from Musali. She has one older brother and three older sisters, all of whom are married into neighboring villages. She got married at the age of 20 and has one son and three daughters. Her father had to take out loans to marry his children. No dowry was involved, but he had to bear marriage expenses.

Her daily routine is similar to all other Vokkaliga women. Since she lives in a nuclear family and her children are very young, she is overworked. She has to work both at home and in the field. She believes that bringing up children in general is hard, it does not matter whether it is a boy or a girl. She thinks that life here is similar to that of the *thavaru*— both families are poor. She had no help while bringing children up. Her father-in-law died seven years ago, and the mother-in-law is living by herself. They were separated fifteen years ago from the joint family. She had to work in the fields even when all her children were small. She goes to *sante* often to buy and sell things. She sells one liter of milk to the dairy every day. She does not go to Hassan frequently, nor does she see any movies. She visits her sisters and brothers. She has many relatives from the husband's side in the village. She takes advice from older women in case children get sick. She does not know anyone who can really lend money in times of trouble. She is not familiar with city life, therefore thinks village life is probably okay, but cannot say for sure. She voted for Congress as her husband and close relatives voted for the same. She is not aware of any laws affecting women. She believes in family planning as she thinks it is a good thing to have small families but she herself has not done anything about it. She says that if she gets pregnant again then she will have the operation as she believes that is the proper time. She thinks it is a good thing to worship the village deity every year as it is good for the village.

She believes that village life is hard on both men and women and even children have to work. She thinks that both men and women are important in village life. She believes that to bring up children properly one should give proper advice; the parents should set an example and correct the children when they go wrong. Decisions about family affairs are made after each consults with the other. The same is true about financial matters. Whatever money they have, they spend it together. She must get permission to go to anybody's place out of the village or to spend money. The husband also informs her if she has to go out of the village and has to spend money on anything in particular.

Dyavamma is rather popular in her residential area. She takes a leading role in organizing activities for various festivals. She was also very helpful to me in mobilizing cooperation by talking to many women. She organized many meetings in her own home. Her help was indispensable for me to make an entry into the community. She is a very hardworking woman. She is very helpful to her neighbors and respected by many. One could see her carrying on conversations with her neighbors about all sorts of things, from child rearing to farm work. She is very proud of herself for being able to make others follow her lead and direction.

Her relationship with her husband is amicable. Neighbors say that they get along well and that she knows how to handle a man. Dyavamma firmly believes that it is up to a woman to make a man behave properly as she can make him or break him. Also, she says that it is a stupid woman who gets beaten up by a man.

She takes care of her children well. She wants them to become educated. She has an only son who has a club foot. She has taken a lot of trouble to get it corrected but hasn't been successful. She is very unhappy that she was so ignorant when the baby was very small and did not do what was necessary right away. Now the doctors say that it is very difficult to correct it.

Her outlook on life is rather philosophical. She feels that she is overworked. Life for her is not very pleasant but full of backbreaking work. She looks forward to the end of the day. She feels that being born a woman is a big burden as life is harder and less fun for them. She says that she wants to be alive until all her children are settled properly, even if it is hard on her.

Appendix B

TABLES

Table 1. Caste, Sex, and Education*

		Illiterate	4	4–7	8–10	10+	Totals
Brahmin	Male	0	10	8	41	16	75
	Female	3	17	7	43	2	72
	Totals	3	27	15	84	18	147
Vokkaliga	Male	23	24	47	43	6	143
	Female	63	25	21	14	0	123
	Totals	86	49	68	57	6	266

*This table shows distribution for the adults of only two castes, Brahmin and Vokkaliga, the two castes we are directly interested in, in this book.

Table 2. Caste and Family Size

Caste	No. of Households	No. of People	Average Family Size
Brahmin	27	157	5.8
Vokkaliga	46	296	6.4
Lingayat	13	66	5.1
Agasa	3	17	5.7
Muslim	7	50	7.1
Scheduled castes	20	113	5.6
Totals	116	699	6.0

Table 3. Average Size of Land Holding and Revenue Payment

Caste	Average Land Holdings (Acres and Gunta*)			Revenue (Rupees and Paise)
	Garden	Wetland	Dry Land	
Brahmin	1A 38½G	2A 30¼G	2A 7¼G	16.06
Vokkaliga	9½G	36¼G	3A 1½G	9.14
Lingayat	14½G	34¾G	1A 20½G	6.92
Muslim	1¾G	10G	34½G	2.40
Scheduled castes	2¼G	21½G	2A 23¼G	4.30

*40 Gunte = 1 Acre.

Table 4. Caste and Education*

Caste	Illiterate	Education in years				Totals
		4	4–7	8–10	10+	
Brahmin	3	27	15	84	18	147
Vokkaliga	86	49	68	57	6	266
Lingayat	12	14	16	16	1	59
Agasa	4	4	1	6	—	15
Muslim	20	12	9	4	—	45
Scheduled Castes	52	14	11	15	1	93
Totals	177	120	120	182	26	625

*For adults

ENDNOTES

CHAPTER I

1. Parashurama (Rama with a *parashu* or *musali*, i.e., axe), one of the great Brahmin sages, did penance in Musali a long time ago to cleanse himself of the evil he had accumulated by killing a number of Kshatriyas. He had to kill these Kshatriyas because they were destroying the Brahminic civilization by their corrupt behavior. After completing the penance, Parashurama was believed to have left his axe behind in the village. The village was named Musali after his weapon. The axe is nowhere to be found now, but people of the village believe in the legend and consider it a holy place.

2. About 25 *paise* more by train in 1977. Rupee is the unit of currency; one rupee is equal to 100 *paise*. Even though in terms of the exchange rate rupee is approximately 1/8 of a dollar, within India its purchasing power is almost the same as that of a dollar in North America.

3. These are called Harijans or untouchables. They are the outcasts of this society.

4. 40 paise for one kg. of wheat, maize, or rice and 20 paise for millet in 1977.

5. Deference customs refer to prescribed behavioral patterns between particular segments of population.

6. There is a general belief among villagers that eating food cooked by lower-caste people—especially the untouchables—and women in their ritually polluted state or touching them causes ritual pollution.

CHAPTER II

1. Beteille and Madan (1975) use these notions to interpret the research experiences of various social scientists.

2. Rabinow (1977) discusses the difficulties involved in penetrating a culture other than one's own and the difficulties involved for the researcher in communicating with the informants because of lack of shared cultural beliefs and symbols and unfamiliarity with the language.

3. There is a strong belief among villagers that physical contact with a lower-caste person pollutes an upper-caste person ritually.

4. Rules of conduct prescribed by tradition.

5. Norma Diamond (1970) writes how she was accorded special status because of her scholarship. She also had problems in gaining access to men's lives just as I did. In addition she had problems in developing rapport with married women as she herself was unmarried.

6. Because of pressure from the state government a woman is elected, but she is discouraged from participation.

7. For example, too much weight should not be put on women's words; men should not start a quarrel with other men based on the information given by women. It is all because women tend to misrepresent and exaggerate the truth.

8. Celebration of the birth of Rama, one of the divine incarnations.

9. The family of orientation.

CHAPTER III

1. Durga is the benevolent manifestation of Goddess Parvati and Kali the malevolent one.

2. The notion of the female being closer to nature is prevalent in other cultures also (Ortner 1973: 67–87).

3. This story is from the Devi Purana and is well known all over India. During the months of September-October, the festival of Durga Puja is celebrated to commemorate this event.

4. This worship is in addition to the annual ceremony in which the entire village participates.

5. The practice of self-immolation of widows.

6. In keeping with such a conception are the views expressed in 1978 by Mr. Morarji Desai, former prime minister of India, referring to the earlier government of Mrs. Indira Gandhi, that too much power in the hands of a woman will lead to a disaster. His statements were given wide publicity in the world press, leading to half-hearted apologies by Mr. Desai.

7. Sita is the wife of Rama, the hero of the epic *Ramayana* and considered to be the incarnation of Vishnu. The epic portrays Sita as making many sacrifices, most willingly, to help her husband Rama achieve his life goals. She is considered as the perfect ideal for all Hindu women to emulate.

8. They are called the *Panchakannikas* or five sacred beings. People of Musali believe that repeating these names at least once every day brings spiritual merit and helps women to model themselves after them.

CHAPTER IV

1. The dynamics of this process are explained in chapter VII.

2. Sex segregation is generally followed in seating arrangements, but there can be exceptions when the children are small.

3. Wife beating in this village seems to be more frequent among Vokkaligas.

4. A discarded wife has a right to maintenance in her husband's house. But her status will be very low, and she just will have to spend her life in the service of others. Rarely does she go to her *thavaru*.

5. Recently laws have been changed to give women the right to divorce, but most people in Musali are unaware of them.

CHAPTER V

1. Widows in general are not allowed to do this since it is believed that they are inauspicious. Among Brahmins those widows who have gone through purification ceremony are excepted.

2. In case one gets contaminated, that is, touched by someone who is not ritually clean—children, people who have not bathed yet, or a Śudra—or an untouchable, a Muslim, or a menstruating woman walks closeby, so as to cast a shadow on the person, then one has to take a bath again and wear another ritually clean *saree*. In case the husband touches the wife, it is considered all right because, to begin with, men are always ritually clean and Agni (the fire God), the ultimate purifier, resides in men's hands. The husband of course is a special case since he is the wife's god personified; he cannot contaminate her in any way.

3. These are festivals signifying various events through the year.

4. The life-style of Gond women as depicted by L. Dube (1975) is very similar to that of the Vokkaliga women reported in this book. Dube's study is one of very few that depicts the life-style of Indian women.

5. This is believed to cool the body system and avoid many illnesses connected with too much "heat" in the body.

CHAPTER VI

1. Ganapathi, or Ganesh, is always worshipped to bring good luck and remove all impediments in achieving a given goal.

2. Since the income is meager, saving this much money is very difficult for an average family after taking care of day-to-day needs. Even those families that are slightly better off take years to save enough money for a marriage.

3. It takes at least three years for a person of Ranga's economic standing to save that much money, if he lives modestly.

4. The horoscopes are almost always matched and marriage performed on auspicious days. There may be exceptions among those who consider themselves very modern.

5. During my visit to Musali in 1983, I found out that after many failures, Padma was finally married to an engineer without parents. Her parents had to pay a dowry of Rs 15,000 and spend another Rs 15,000 in marriage expenses.

6. This is becoming important in some Vokkaliga families also where the sons and daughters are educated.

7. Among Brahmins, if the marriage is between village dwellers the physical strength of the man but not that of the woman is considered important.

CHAPTER VII

1. The descriptions given here share a remarkable similarity with Oscar Lewis's description of sex in cultures of poverty (1966).

2. This incident took place in Icnalli, a village fifteen miles from Musali.

3. Some of the strategies that could be used in such contexts are very reminiscent of Morgan's discussion in *The Total Woman* (1973).

4. Currently laws have been passed to make bigamy illegal, but they are taking effect only slowly.

5. Roy (1975) in her study of Bengali women observes that religion provides much solace and comfort to women who feel very dissatisfied with their lives.

6. This incident took place in Musali around 1949.

CHAPTER VIII

1. Dubois in her study (1944) observes that women of Alor are slow, submissive, less intelligent, humble, nurturant, industrious, and given to following routine. She also writes that they are neither curious nor striving. Women of Musali resemble the women of Alor in many respects.

2. *Vadhuvige Kivimathu*, a popular guide to marriage, given as present during marriage, exemplifies this.

3. I do not agree with Kakar when he writes that " . . . in infancy, the most radical period of emotional development, Indian girls are assured of their worth by whom it really matters: by their mothers" (1978:60).

CHAPTER IX

1. There were some exceptions to this rule in parts of India, for example, among the Nayars of Mallabar (Fuller 1976: 56–63).

2. Except for *stridhana*, that is, personal gifts, like jewelry, clothing, etc., received from kith and kin.

3. Altekar writes, "Husband was to be considered a wife's personal god" (1956: 355). Upadhyaya writes, "The social adjustment of the sexes was so perfect that we find no complaint on the part of the women against the authority of the man" (1974: 220).

4. The rules were not as strict in the lower castes, among whom remarriage of widows, especially those without children, was accepted (Thompson 1928; Altekar:1956). But in their attempt to achieve upward mobility, the lower castes adopted upper-caste behavioral patterns, referred to as Sanskritization (Srinivas 1968).

5. Altekar writes that "society had a general prejudice against female education; it was believed that a girl taught to read and write would become a widow" (1956: 24).

6. Rise of Buddhism and Jainism (seventh to fifth centuries B.C.) and Bhakti Era (eleventh to fifteenth centuries, A.D.).

7. During the Bhakti era, that is, between eleventh to fifteenth centuries A.D., devotee Akkamahadevi is said to have lived in South India while devotee Meera lived in the North.

8. For example, in films such as *Subah* (*Morning*) the heroine rejects the ideal of Pativratya and chooses to live her life as a social worker.

SELECTED BIBLIOGRAPHY

Agnew, Vijay. *Elite Women in Indian Politics*. New Delhi: Vikas Publishing House, 1979.

Agrawala, V. (trans.). *The Glorification of the Great Goddess* (The Devi Mahatmya). Banaras: All India Kashiraj Trust, 1963.

Allen, Michael, and Mukherjee, S. N. *Women in India and Nepal*. Canberra, Australia: ANU Printing for the South Asian History, 1982.

Altekar, A. S. *The Position of Women in Hindu Civilisation*. Banaras: Motilal Banarsidass, 1956.

Asthana, Pratima. *Women's Movement in India*. Delhi: Vikas Publishing House, 1974.

Babb, Lawrence A. *The Divine Hierarchy: Popular Hinduism in Central India*. New York: Columbia University Press, 1975.

Beals, Alan R. *Gopalpur: A South Indian Village*. New York: Holt, Rinehart & Winston, 1962.

————. *Village Life in South India*. Chicago: Aldine, 1974.

Beck, Brenda E. *Peasant Society in Konku*. Vancouver, B.C.: University of British Columbia Press, 1972.

Bell, Robert R., and Gordon, Michael. *The Social Dimensions of Human Sexuality*. Boston: Little, Brown. 1972.

Bellah, R. (ed). *Religion and Progress in Modern Asia*. Glencoe, Ill.: Free Press, 1965.

Benedict, Ruth. *Patterns of Culture*. Boston: Houghton Mifflin, 1946.

Beneria, Lourdes, and Sen, Gita. "Accumulation, Reproduction and Women's Role in Economic Development: Boserup Revised." *SIGNS: Journal of Women in Culture and Society* (Winter 1981): 279–98.

Bennett, Lynn. *Dangerous Wives and Sacred Sisters*. New York: Columbia University Press, 1983.

Bernstein, Basil. "A Public Language: Some Sociological Implications of a Linguistic Form." *British Journal of Sociology* 10 (1957): 311–26.

Beteille, André. *Class, Caste and Power*. Berkeley, Cal.: University of California Press, 1965.

Beteille, André, and Madan, T. N. (eds.). *Encounter and Experience*. Delhi: Vikas Publishing House, 1975.

Bose, N. K. *Culture and Society in India*. Bombay: Asia Publishing House, 1967.

Bruner, Jerome. *Studies in Cognitive Growth*. New York: John Wiley & Sons, 1966.

Buhler, G. (trans.). *The Laws of Manu*. vol. 25. *Sacred Books of the East*, M. Muller, ed. Oxford: Clarendon Press of Oxford University Press, 1886.

Carstairs, M. *Twice Born*. Bloomington, Ind.: Indiana University Press, 1961.

Cohen, Y. A. *Social Structure and Personality*. New York: Holt, Rinehart & Winston, 1961.

Conklin, G. H. "Cultural Determinants of Power for Women within the Family." *Journal of Comparative Family Studies* X (1979): 35–53.

Daly, Mary. *Beyond God the Father*. Boston: Beacon Press, 1973.

Dasgupta, S. *A History of Indian Philosophy*. Cambridge, Eng.: Cambridge University Press, 1963.

Davies, M. (ed.). *Third World: Second Sex*. London: Zed Press, 1983.

de Souza, A. (ed.). *Women in Contemporary India*. New Delhi: Manohar Book Service, 1975.

Diamond, Norma. "Fieldwork in a Complex Society: Taiwan." In *Being an Anthropoligist*. G. D. Spindler, ed. New York: Holt, Rinehart & Winston, 1970.

Douglas, Mary. *Implicit Meanings: Essays in Anthropology*. London: Routledge & Kegan Paul, 1975.

Dube, Leela. "Women's Worlds—Three Encounters." In *Encounter and Experience*. A. Beteille and T. N. Madan, eds. Delhi: Vikas Publishing House, 1975.

Dube, S. C. *India's Changing Villages*. London: Routledge & Kegan Paul, 1958.

DuBois, C. *The People of Alor*. Minneapolis, Minn.: The University of Minnesota Press, 1944.

Dumont, Louis. *Homo Hierarchicus*. Chicago: University of Chicago Press, 1970.

Durkheim, Émile. *The Elementary Forms of Religious Life*. Glencoe, Ill: Free Press, 1965.

————. *The Division of Labor in Society*. (1893). G. Simpson, trans. Glencoe, Ill.: Free Press, 1964.

Dyson, Tim, and Crook, Nigel. *India's Demography: Essays on the Contemporary Populations*. New Delhi: South Asian Publishers, 1984.

Epstein, Scarlett T. *South India: Yesterday, Today and Tomorrow*. New York: Holmes & Meier, 1973.

Erikson, Erik H. *Gandhi's Truth*. New York: Norton, 1969.

Everett, Jana. "Approaches to the 'Women's Question' in India: From Maternalism to Mobilization." *Women's Studies International Quarterly* 4 (1981): 169–78.

Fuller, C. J. *The Nayars Today*. London: Cambridge University Press, 1976.

Fruzzetti, Lina M. *The Gift of a Virgin: Women, Marriage, and Ritual in a Bengali Society*. New Brunswick, N.J.: Rutgers University Press, 1982.

Gagne, R. M. "Contribution of Learning to Human Development." *Psychological Review* 75 (1968): 177–91.

Geertz, Clifford. *Interpretations of Culture*. New York: Basic Books, 1973.

Gergen, Kenneth J., and Marlowe, David. *Personality and Social Behaviour*. Don Mills, Ont.: Addison-Wesley, 1970.

Giddens, Anthony (ed.). *Durkheim, E.: Selected Writings*. Cambridge, Eng.: Cambridge University Press, 1972.

Goldberg, P. "Are Women Prejudiced Against Women." *Transaction* 5 (1968): 28–30.

Goldstein, Rhoda L. *Indian Women in Transition: A Bangalore Case Study*. Metuchen, N. J.: Scarecrow Press, 1972.

Gore, Mrinal S. *Urbanization and Family Change*. Bombay: Popular Prakashan, 1968.

Greenfield, P. M., and J. S. Bruner. "Culture and Cognitive Growth." In *Handbook of Socialization Theory and Research*, D. A. Goslin, ed. Chicago: Rand-McNally College Publishing, 1969.

Haan, Norma. *Coping and Defending*. New York: Academic Press, 1977.

Hate, Chandrakala A. *Changing Status of Women*. Bombay: Allied Publishing, 1969.

Horner, M. S. "Toward an Understanding of Achievement-Related Conflicts in Women." *Journal of Social Issues* 28 (1972): 157–75.

Hsu, F. L. K. (ed.). *Psychological Anthropology.* Cambridge, Mass.: Schenkman, 1972.

ICSSR. *Status of Women Report.* New Delhi: Allied Publishers, 1975.

Inkeles, Alex, and Levinson, D. J. "Rational Character: The Study of Moral Personality and Sociocultural Systems." In *The Handbook of Social Psychology,* 2nd ed., vol. 4, G. Lindsey and E. Aronson, eds. London: Addison-Wesley, 1968.

Inkeles, Alex, and Smith, D. H. *Becoming Modern.* Cambridge Mass.: Harvard University Press, 1974.

Ishwaran, K. *Shivapur: A South Indian Village.* London: Routledge & Kegan Paul, 1968.

Jacobson, Doranne, and Wadley, Susan S. *Women in India: Two Perspectives.* New Delhi: Manohar, 1977.

Jain, Devaki. *Women's Quest for Power.* Ghaziabad, Utter Pradesh: Vikas Publishing House, 1980.

Kakar, Sudhir. *The Inner World.* Oxford and New York: Oxford University Press, 1978.

Kane, P. V. *History of Dharmasastra.* 5 vols. Poona: Bhandarkar Oriental Institute, 1938–58.

Kapadia, K. M. *Marriage and Family in India.* 2nd. ed. Oxford: Oxford University Press, 1958.

Kapur, Promilla. *Marriage and Working Women in India.* Delhi: Vikas Publications, 1970.

Kardiner, A. *The Individual and His Society.* New York: Columbia University Press, 1939.

Karve, Irawati. *Group Relations in Village Community.* Madras: G. S. Press, 1963.

Kelly, M. P. F. "Development and the Sexual Division of Labor: An Introduction." *SIGNS: Journal of Women in Culture and Society* 7 (Winter 1981): 268–78.

Kishwar, Madhu, and Vanita, Ruth. "Using Women As A Pretext For Repression." *Manushi* 37 (1986):2–8.

Kluckhohn, Florence, and Strodtbeck, Fred L. *Variations in Value Orientations.* Evanston, Ill.: Row, Peterson, 1961.

Kohlberg, Lawrence K. "Stage and Sequence: The Cognitive-Developmental Approach to Socialization." In *Handbook of Socialization: Theory and Research.* D. A. Goslin, ed. New York: Rand-McNally, 1969.

Kohn, Melvin L., and Schooler, Carmi. "The Reciprocal Effects of the Substantive Complexity of Work and Intellectual Flexibility: A Longitudinal Assessment." *American Journal of Sociology* 84 (1978): 24–52.

Komarovsky, Mirra. "Cultural Contradictions and Sex Roles." *American Journal of Sociology* 52 (1946): 182–89.

Lebra, Joyce, Poulson, Joy, and Everett, Jana (eds). *Women and Work in India: Continuity and Change*. New Delhi: Promilla, 1984.

Levine, Donald N. *Georg Simmel: On Individuality and Social Form*. Chicago: University of Chicago Press, 1971.

Levine, Robert A. *Culture, Behavior and Personality*. Chicago: Aldine, 1973.

————. *Culture and Personality: Contemporary Readings*. Chicago: Aldine, 1974.

Levy, R. *Tahitians*. Chicago: University of Chicago Press, 1973.

Lewis, Oscar. "The Culture of Poverty." *Scientific American*, Oct. 1966.

Loevinger, Jane. *Ego Development: Conceptions and Theories*. San Francisco: Jossey-Bass, 1976.

Lukes, Steven (ed.). *Émile Durkheim, His life and Work: A Historical and Critical Study*. London: Allen Lane, 1973.

Luschinsky, Mildred S. "The Impact of Some Recent Indian Government Legislation on the Women of an Indian Village." *Asian Survey* 3 (1963): 573–83.

McClelland, David, and Winter, D. C. *Motivating Economic Achievement*. Toronto, Ont.: Collier-Macmillan Canada, 1969.

Madan, T. N. "The Hindu Women at Home." In *Indian Women*, B. R. Nanda, ed. New Delhi: Vikas Publishing House, 1976.

Mandelbaum, David C. *Society in India*. Chicago: University of Chicago Press, 1955.

Marchak, Patricia M. *Ideological Perspectives on Canada*. Toronto: McGraw-Hill Ryerson, 1975.

Marriott, McKim. "The Feast of Love." In *Krishna: Myths, Rites, and Attitude*, M. Singer, ed. Honolulu: East-West Center Press, 1966.

————. "Hindu Transactions: Diversity without Dualism." In *Transaction and Meaning*, B. Kapferer, ed. Philadelphia: Institute for the Study of Human Issues, 1976.

Mathur, K. S. *Caste and Ritual in a Malwa Village*. New York: Asia Publishing House, 1964.

Mazumdar, V. "The Social Reform Movement in India—From Ranade to Nehru." In *Indian Women*, B. R. Nanda, ed. New Dehli: Vikas Publishing House, 1976.

Mead, George H. *Mind, Self, and Society*. Chicago: University of Chicago Press, 1934.

Mead, Margaret. "An Investigation of the Thought of Primitive Children, with Special Reference to Animism." *Journal of the Royal Anthropological Institute* 62 (1932): 173–90.

————. *Coming of Age in Samoa*. New York: Morrow, 1928.

Mies, Maria. *The Lace Makers of Narsapur*. London: Zed Press, 1982.

Miller, Barbara D. *The Endangered Sex: Neglect of Female Children in Rural North India*. Ithaca, N. Y.: Cornell University Press, 1981.

Miller, D, and Swanson, G. *The Changing American Parent*. New York: Wiley, 1958.

Minturn, L., and Hitchcock, J. T. *The Rajputs of Khalapur*. New York: John Wiley, 1966.

Mischel, Walter. *Personality and Assessment*. New York: Wiley, 1968.

————. "Toward a Cognitive Social Learning Reconceptualization of Personality." *Psychology Review* 80 (1973): 252–79.

Moodey, R. W. *Masculinity and Feminity Among Students in Delhi and Jaipur*. Ph.D. Diss., University of Chicago, 1971.

Morgan, Marabel. *The Total Woman*. Markham, Ont.: Fleming H. Revell, Simon & Schuster of Canada, 1973.

Nanda, B.R. (ed.) *Indian Women: From Purdah to Modernity*. Bangalore: Vikas Publishing House, 1976.

Narain, R. K. *Gods, Demons, and Others*. London: William Heinemann, 1964.

Nehru, Jawaharlal. *The Discovery of India*. London: Meridian Books, 1951.

Niranjana, A. *Vadhuvige, Kivimathu (Kannada)*. Mysore: D. V. K. Murthy, 1977.

Nisbet, Robert A. *The Sociology of Émile Durkheim*. New York: Oxford University Press, 1974.

Obeysekere, B. "Pregnancy Cravings (Dola-Duka) in Relation to Social Structure and Personality in a Sinhalese Village." In *Culture and Personality, Contemporary Readings*, R. A. Levine, ed. Chicago: Aldine, 1974.

Omvedt, Gail. *We Will Smash This Prison! Indian Women in Struggle*. London: Zed Press, 1980.

Ortner, Sherry B. "Is Female to Male as Nature is to Culture?" In *Women, Culture, and Society*, M. Z. Rosaldo, and L. Lamphere, eds. Stanford, Calif.: Stanford University Press, 1973.

Parrinder, G. *The Bhagavad Gita: A Verse Translation*. London: Sheldon Press, 1974.

Parsons, Talcott. *The Social System*. New York: Free Press, 1961.

Pearlin, L. I., and Kohn, Melvin L. "Social Class, Occupation, and Values: A Cross National Study." *American Sociological Review* 31 (1966): 466–79.

Pearson, G. "The Female Intelligentsia in Segregated Society: Early 20th Century Bombay." In *Women in India and Nepal*, M. Allen and S. N. Mukherjee, eds. Canberra, Australia: ANU printing for South Asian History, 1982.

Piaget, J. "Need and Significance of Cross Cultural Studies in Genetic

Psychology, 1966." In *Culture and Cognition Readings in Cross Cultural Psychology*, J. W. Berry and P. R. Dasen, eds. London: Methuen, 1974.

Poster, Mark. *Critical Theory of the Family*. New York: Seabury Press, 1978.

Rabinow, Paul. *Reflections on Field-Work in Morocco*. Berkeley: University of California Press, 1977.

Radhakrishnan, Sarvapalli, and Moore, C. A. (eds.). *A Source Book in Indian Philosophy*. Princeton, N. J.: Princeton University Press, 1957.

Rao, Usha. *Women in a Developing Society*. New Delhi: Ashish Publishing House, 1983.

Research Unit on Women's Studies. *Women in India*. Bombay: S.N.D.T. Women's University, 1975.

Rocher, Guy. *A General Introduction to Sociology*. Toronto: Macmillan, 1972.

Ross, Aileen D. *The Hindu Family in Urban Setting*. Toronto: University of Toronto Press, 1961.

Roy, Manisha. *Bengali Women*. Chicago: University of Chicago Press, 1975.

Roy, P. C. (trans.). *The Mahabharatha*. 12 vols. Calcutta: Oriental Publishing Co., n.d.

Rudolph, Lloyd I., and Rudolph, H. R. *The Modernity of Tradition*. Chicago: University of Chicago Press, 1967.

Safa, Helen I., and Leacock, Eleanor. "Development and the Sexual Division of Labor." *SIGNS: Journal of Women in Culture and Society* (Winter 1981): 418–33.

Safilios-Rothschild, Constantina. *Toward a Sociology of Women*. Toronto: Xerox College Publishing, 1972.

Sahlins, Marshall. *Culture and Practical Reason*. Chicago: University of Chicago Press, 1976.

Selman, R. L., and Kohlberg, Lawrence. *The Relation of Stages of Social Role-taking to Moral Development: A Theoretical and Empirical Analysis*. Unpublished ms., Harvard University, 1973.

Sengupta, Padmini. *Story of Women in India*. New Delhi: Indian Book Co., 1974.

Shibutani, T. *Society and Personality*. Englewood Cliffs, N. J.: Prentice Hall, 1961.

Shils, Edward. *Selected Essays*. Chicago: University of Chicago Press, 1970.

———. *The Intellectual Between Tradition and Modernity: The Indian Situation*. The Hague: Mouton, 1961.

Singer, Milton. *Traditional India: Structure and Change*. Philadelphia: American Folklore Society, 1959.

———. *When a Great Tradition Modernizes*. New York: Praeger, 1972.

Smith, M. B. "Competence and Socialization." In *Socialization and Society*, J. A. Clausen, ed. Boston: Little, Brown, 1968.

Spiro, Melford E. *Buddhism and Society*. Evanston, Ill.: Harper & Row, 1970.

———. *Context and Meaning in Cultural Anthropology*. New York: Free Press, 1970.

Spratt, P. *Hindu Culture and Personality*. Bombay: Manaktalas, 1966.

Srinivas, M. N. *Religion and Society Among the Coorgs of South India*. Oxford: Clarendon Press, 1952.

———. *Social Change in Modern India*. Berkeley: University of California Press, 1968.

———. *The Remembered Village*. Berkeley: University of California Press, 1976.

Srinivas, M. N. (ed.). *Caste in Modern India*. New York: Asia Publishing House, 1962.

Strodtbeck, Fred L. "Hidden Curriculum in the Middle-Class Home." In *Learning and the Educational Process*, J. D. Drumboltz, ed. Chicago: Rand-McNally, 1965.

———. "Tutoring and Psychological Growth." In *Children as Teachers*, V. L. Allen, ed. New York: Academic Press, 1975.

Suzman, R. M. "Psychological Modernity." *International Journal of Comparative Sociology* 14 (1973): 173–387.

Thomas, P. *Indian Women Through The Ages*. Bombay: Asia Publishing House, 1964.

Turner, Victor W. *The Ritual Process*. Chicago: Aldine, 1969.

Upadhyaya, B. S. *Women in Rigveda*. Bombay: S. Chand, 1974.

Vivekananda, S. *The Complete Works of Swami Vivekananda*. 8 vols. Calcutta: Advaita Ashrama, 1962–70.

Weber, Max. *The Religion of India*. Toronto: Collier-Macmillan Canada, 1958.

Whiting, J. M., and Child, I. L. *Child Training and Personality: A Cross-Cultural Study*. New York: Yale University Press, 1953.

Wilson, Monica. *Rituals of Kinship Among the Nyakyusa*. London: Published for the International African Institute by the Oxford University Press, 1957.

Wiser, William H., and Wiser, Charlotte V. *Behind Mud Walls*. Berkeley: University of California Press, 1971.

Wolf, M. *Women and the Family in Rural Taiwan*. Stanford, Calif.: Stanford Universtiy Press, 1972.

Wolff, Kurt H. *The Sociology of Georg Simmel*. Glencoe, Ill.: Free Press, 1950.

The Wellesley Editorial Committee. *Women and National Development: The Complexities of Change*. Chicago: University of Chicago Press, 1977.

Index

Agnew, 114
Agrawala, 30
Alcohol consumption, 8, 45
Allen and Mukharjee, 31, 33
Altekar, 32, 69, 111
Androcentric ideology, 107, 108
Anuloma, 2
Araike, 66, 67, 70, 88
Arathi, 88
Ardhangi, 37
Arecanut, curing and processing, 52
Arranged marriage, 29, 37, 69–73, 76–78, 118
Aryan wife, 111
Asthana, 119, 120
Autonomy and self-direction, 103, 104, 105

Babb, 30
Bad spirits, 62
Beedi, 6
Behavioral prescriptions, 99
Beliefs, 63–64, 68. *See also* Normative beliefs
Beneria and Sen, 115
Betel leaves, 55
Bhakti era, 156n
Bhakti movement, and women, 110
Birth of a daughter, 61, 62
Bossiness, 43, 46
Bride price, 9, 37

Buddhism and Jainism, 156n
Buhler, 29, 30, 110

Carstairs, 36, 41, 42, 59
Caste, 2, 3, 8, 9, 10, 11, 13, 20, 27, 29, 105, 151
   (table)
Chatting and favorite topics, 55, 56
Childbirth, 88–89
Children, caring for, 51–52
Chutni, 50
Conformity, enforcement of, 59, 60
Conklin, 117
Conservative forces, 112
Constitution of free India, 112
Curriculum, in colleges, 113

Daily chores, 50–51
Daly, 34
Dasgupta, 30
Dasokkalu, 15, 16
Daughters, 60–61, 77, 78, 105–6, 118
Davies, 120
Deference customs, 8, 9, 40–42, 104
Depersonalization, 99
de Souza, 112, 120
Destiny of women, 112
Devi Purana, 153n
Dharma, 20

Diamond, 153n
Discrimination, 113
Double bind, 116
Douglas, 29
Dowry, 9, 37, 106, 118
Dualistic conception, 29
Durga Mata, 111
Durkheim, 99
Dwijas, 2
Dyson and Crook, 88

Economic well-being, 151 (table)
Economic structure, 3–5
Education, 1, 2, 78, 112, 151 (table)
Ekadashi, 56
Electrification, 19
Elite women, 114
Emotional affinity, 46
Endogamy, 36
Epics and Puranas, 32
Epstein, 36
Equality for women, 116, 117
Everett, 120

Family, average size of, 150 (table)
Family structure, 35, 109
Female infanticide, 111
Festivals, 11, 52, 53
Films, 156n

Ganhi, Indira, 111, 153n
Gender stereotyping, 115, 116
Ghee, 50, 66
Goddesses, 30
Goldstein, 78, 113, 121
Gossip, 43
Gramadevatha, 7, 9, 11, 31. *See also* Village
    goddess
Gummayya, 59

Handicrafts, 56–57
Harikathas, 32, 56
Health care, 63, 101, 114
Henpecked, 47
Hindu philosophy, ix
Hindu reformers, 111
Hittu, 51, 53
Home wreckers, 39
Horoscopes, 155n
Housework, sharing of, 52, 54
Husband-wife relationship, 39, 41, 46, 47–48,
    82, 106

ICSSR, 89, 112, 113, 114, 118
Illiteracy, 112
Independence struggle, 74
Institutional structure, 99

Jacobson and Wadley, 29, 111
Jain, 115, 116, 117
Jāti, 2, 3, 10, 12, 15
Joint family, 35–36
Jokes, 47–48

Kaddi-Pudi, 55
Kanya dana, 69
Kapur, 39, 114, 117
Karve, 38
Kelly, 116, 118
Kishwar and Vanita, 120
Krishna, 63
Kudike, 95
Kumkum, 49, 93

Labor: productive, 53–54; reproductive, 54
Lakshmi, 37
Language, 8
Laws about women, 36, 115, 154n
Lebra et al., 112, 113, 114, 115
Levine, 103
Life-cycle ceremonies, 12, 16, 20, 60–61,
    62–63, 65–66, 79–81
Lingayat, 10
Literacy, 113, 150 (table). *See also* Illiteracy
Loyalty, 107
Luschinsky, 36, 115

Madan, 117
Mahabharatha, 110
Mahila Samaj, 13
Majjige, 50
Manu, 30, 110
Marchak, 26
Marital adjustment, 114
Marriage, 45, 69, 118. *See also* Arranged
    marriage; Bride price; Dowry
Marriage ceremony, 79–81
Marriage manuals, 114, 155n
Mazumdar, 117
Meat consumption, 53–54
Menstruation, 65, 67–68. *See also* Pollution
Men's work, 55
Methods of social control, 99, 100
Midday meal, 51

Mies, 116, 117
Milk cooperative, 17
Miller, 118
Minturn and Hitchcock, 36, 59
Modernization, 1, 112
Mosaru, 50
Mother-in-law and daughter-in-law, 36, 44–45, 55, 107
Mother-son relationship, 45
Mother's love, 44, 96, 97
Mothers, 44–45, 87–88, 107, 119
Mullokkalu, 15, 16
Musali, 152n
Muthaidēs, 96, 99

Nanda, 112, 119
Nayars of Mallabar, 155n
Nehru, Jawaharlal, 112
Niranjana, 114
Noga, 79
Normative beliefs, 98–99. *See also* Pativratya
Nuclear family, 120. *See also* Family structure

Occupation, 5
Old age, 89–91
Omvedt, 120

Padmini, 84–85
Paise, 152n
Panchayat, 12–13, 14, 21
Pativrata, 26–27, 31, 32, 33, 45, 98, 101
Pativratya, 26–34, 45, 58, 98–101, 106, 109, 114
Patterns of adaptation, 101–3
Pearson, 111
Personal goals, 99
Physical abuse, 46, 48
Physical strength, 43
Political processes, 113, 114
Pollution, 2, 11, 20, 27, 29, 30, 31, 67
Pool of eligibles, 76. *See also* Arranged marriage
Power, 2, 8, 13, 15, 21, 24–25, 38
Pratiloma, 2
Prejudice, against women's education, 156n
Professional women, 113
Puja, 50
Purdah, 111
Purification of widows, 31, 93–94

Rabinow, 153n
Radhakrishnan and Moore, 30

Ranganathananda, 31, 32
Rangole, 49
Rao, 118
Rebirth, 96
Religion, 7
Remarriage of widows, 156n
Research Unit on Women's Studies, 113, 118, 120
Rishi Panchami, 68
Ritual purity, 50, 52, 154n
Ross, 44, 120
Rotti, 50, 53
Roy, 110

Safa and Leacock, 115
Sanskritization, 9–10
Sati, 31, 32, 100, 111
Scheduled castes, 2, 8, 9, 10, 11, 21. *See also* Untouchables
Self-denigrating rituals, 47, 100
Self-esteem, 100, 117
Self-image, 103
Self-realization, 99
Sengupta, 33, 109, 111
Sense of belonging, 81–83
Sex, 83–87
Sex ratio, 114
Sex segregation, of children, 65, 154n
Shakti, 30
Single women, 112, 113
Sita, 32
Social distance, 46, 105
Social status, 8–9
Socialization, 58–60
Sociocultural milieu, 3
Solidarity, 105–6, 120
Sons, 45, 60, 61, 88, 89, 118, 119
Special meals, 52, 53
Srinivas, 9, 17, 37
Stages of life cycle. *See* various entries
Status of women, 109, 110
Status of Women Report, 113
Stridhana, 155n
Structural conditions, 109
Structural needs, 99
Struggle for independence, 117
System of symbols, 99

Tamarind, 50, 52
Teetotalers, 8
Temples, 7
Thavaru, 25, 55, 73, 81, 82, 83, 105, 107
Thomas, 109

Threshold, cleaning and decorating of, 49, 52
Toddy, 8
Turner, 99

Untouchables, 2, 21. *See also* Scheduled castes
Upadhyaya, 109
Upanishads, 32, 109
Urban families, 121
Ushli, 62

Vedas, 32, 109
Vegetarian diet, 8, 105
Vijnana, 30
Village goddess, 30. *See also* Gramadevatha

Violence against women, 22, 43, 46–48, 82–83, 154n
Vivekananda, 33

Wages, 56, 57
Widowhood, 91–96, 109
Widows, 31, 91–95, 106, 111, 154n
Wilson, 98
Wiser and Wiser, 36, 41, 42, 62
Womanhood, training for, 65–67
Women, ix, 27, 28, 31, 32, 36, 38, 43, 44, 47, 85, 87, 99, 100–1, 107, 109, 117, 119
Women's associations, 120
Women's claim for equality, 119
Women's identity, 99
Women's liberation movement, 119, 120
Women's work, 55, 100, 116